SOCIAL WORK AND LAW

HOUSING: SECURITY
AND
RENT CONTROL

AUSTRALIA
The Law Book Company Ltd.
Sydney: Melbourne: Brisbane

CANADA AND U.S.A.
The Carswell Company Ltd.
Agincourt, Ontario

INDIA
N.M. Tripathi Private Ltd.
Bombay
and
Eastern Law House Private Ltd.
Calcutta
M.P.P. House
Bangalore

ISRAEL
Steimatzyky's Agency Ltd.
Jerusalem: Tel Aviv: Haifa

MALAYSIA: SINGAPORE: BRUNEI
Malayan Law Journal (Pte.) Ltd.
Singapore

NEW ZEALAND
Sweet and Maxwell (N.Z.) Ltd.
Wellington

PAKISTAN
Pakistan Law House
Karachi

SOCIAL WORK AND LAW

HOUSING: SECURITY AND RENT CONTROL

ANDREW ARDEN, LL.B.
Barrister

LONDON
SWEET AND MAXWELL
1978

Published in 1978 by
Sweet & Maxwell Ltd. of
11 New Fetter Lane, London.
Photoset by Red Lion Setters, London.
Printed in Great Britain by
Fletcher & Son Ltd., Norwich

ISBN 0 421 23670 1

Preface

A number of people have helped, directly or indirectly, in preparing this book. In particular, Ian Bynoe, Hilary Fassnidge, David Harter, Ruth Lister, Maggie Rae and Jo Tunnard have commented on individual sections. It would not be right for me to ignore the indirect contribution made by those with whom I have worked in housing law over a number of years: Tony Gifford, Martin Partington and my colleagues, past and present, at the Legal Action Group. To adopt the refreshingly blunt expression used by Brenda Hoggett in her Preface to *Parents and Children*, also in this series: "I am grateful to everyone: it is certainly no one's fault but my own if I have got it wrong."

The law in this book applies only to England and Wales. It was written and is intended to be read as a companion volume to the work *Housing: Repairs and Improvements* by Tom Hadden. This book, therefore, does not touch upon housing conditions at all. The law is up-to-date to 1 April 1978.

ANDREW ARDEN

Contents

TABLE OF CASES

References are given to the most accessible reports of cases referred to in text. Abbreviations used:

TABLE OF STATUTES

1 An Introduction to Housing Law

The need for shelter is one of the most basic of all human needs. Put another way around, everybody needs somewhere to live. The arrangements which people make to fulfill this need are many and varied: some people own their own homes, whether houses or flats, and whether outright or under mortgage; some rent from a private, professional landlord, others from a public authority; some live with family, others with friends; some rent a furnished room, perhaps in a hotel or hostel, perhaps in a house of bedsitting-rooms; some are provided with meals by their landlords, others cook for themselves; some can find or afford nowhere to buy or rent and so "squat" in empty houses. The list is endless and limited only by the scope of human imagination at a time that is generally recognised to be one of major shortages of adequate quality housing stock.

Housing law is about the regulation of these accommodation arrangements. It touches every member of society, in one way or another and with different degrees of directness. As such, it ought to be a subject as comfortably within the grasp of, at the least, most members of society, as are the basic tenents of, *e.g.* the criminal law.

This, however, is very far from being the case. Housing law is one of the most complex of all legal studies. There are many reasons why this is so and they are worth considering at the outset so that the reader may anticipate the complexities he will be required to study:

(i) *Changing patterns*

When patterns of housing change, the basic material of the study is itself in flux. If you like, the facts to which the law relates are different. This frequently leads to the application of anachronistic laws to modern situations. For example, many more young people today leave the family home to set up house for themselves before marriage than used to be the case. Commonly, they will share a house or a flat with others. To deal with this situation, all that the law can draw upon is a fairly ancient body of rules built up in connection with joint, family occupation of land. This body of law was intended to deal with far more stable occupation arrangements than most flat-shares turn out to be.

Landlords, too, change their letting habits, although usually for a rather different reason: in order to fit contemporary housing legislation. For example, before the First World War, furnished accommodation was a comparative luxury. During the First World War, the first of the modern protective Acts of Parliament was passed to protect unfurnished tenants. As a result, by the end of the Second World War, furnished lettings had become common and by the time that the law relating to furnished lettings was changed in 1974, it had become virtually impossible to rent unfurnished accommodation at all.

Social policies also change. In 1914, 10 per cent. of the population lived in owner-occupied property while the remaining 90 per cent. occupied property rented from private landlords. In 1976, 55 per cent. of the housing stock was owner-occupied, 15 per cent. rented from private landlords, and 30 per cent. rented from what are commonly called the public and quasi-public landlords, such as local authorities, housing associations, etc.

The net result of these changes is that anyone who seeks to grasp what is relevant in housing law has to be aware of the old, common law (see below) rules relating to landlord and tenant, of modern protective legislation affecting the tenants of private landlords, of the law as it has developed in relation to the tenants of local authorities, of the elements of protection which apply to the tenants of housing associations, and, indeed, of the laws governing the relationship between a mortgage company and an owner-occupier who has taken out a mortgage with which to buy his home, as will frequently be the case.

(ii) *Sources of law*

Some of the different sources of law have already been mentioned. It is a matter of general knowledge that much law comes from Acts of Parliament. Most people also know that Acts of Parliament have frequently to be interpreted by the courts, because they are not unequivocally clear or because they do not appear to deal with a particular situation. This means that a body of case law quickly builds up in relation to these Acts. But in addition, there is what is known as the common law. This is the basic law (or rules of society) which has never been set out in any Act of Parliament, but which has been declared as law in the reports of court cases stretching back for hundreds of years. Common law has the same degree of force as any other law, although statutes (Acts of Parliament) may change the common law, just as one Act of Parliament may alter an earlier Act.

These sources of law do not stand independently of each other. Acts of Parliament deal with situations, themselves described or defined by the common law. A reported decision on an Act of Parliament may at one and the same time establish the limits of that Act, and alter what has hitherto been understood to be the common law. These sources cannot be regarded as simply different places from which to extract rules and regulations, but, rather, as the poles of a dynamic field of study.

(iii) *Divergence between law and language*

Probably the most important single reason why a person approaching housing law for the first time will find it difficult, is because of the divergence between the language of law and that which is in popular use. For example, the term bedsitting-room will be used popularly to describe a single, rented, usually furnished room. In law, however, the bedsitting-room may be occupied under a tenancy, or else it may be under a lesser form a contractual arrangement, closer to that non-contractual permission which a child has to live in the home of his parents, known as licence: *Marchant* v. *Charters*.

The term "squatter" is one which is popularly used to apply to those living in someone else's property without permission, and also to anyone living in what is known as short-life property, *i.e.* property due for demolition or redevelopment. But squatters, too, may be licensees, or they may be trespassers. The terms landlord and tenant are themselves used commonly to describe anyone who rents out accommodation and anyone who lives in accommodation belonging to another, paying rent for it. But just who is, and who is not, a tenant can be a matter of some considerable finesse.

(iv) *The content of the laws*

The last of the factors which we shall consider here by way of introduction to the basic material of housing law is the content of the laws themselves. We shall take a closer look below at some of these laws, and, of course, a detailed look at the most important laws throughout the rest of the book. For the moment, it is worth remarking that the laws themselves often appear to lack any rationality, rhyme or reason. The main body of protective legislation is known as the Rent Acts, and this was recently consolidated into a single, Rent Act 1977. It limits the rent which a landlord may lawfully charge a tenant, and it prevents a landlord from evicting a tenant except on certain, limited grounds. These provisions apply regardless of what the parties have agreed between themselves.

But not all tenants are protected by the Acts. They were not originally intended to cover luxury accommodation, *e.g.* furnished accommodation as it was used at the beginning of the century; accommodation where services are provided by the landlord; accommodation in large and expensive houses in the wealthiest parts of a town. Similarly, the Act does not now cover the tenants of resident landlords, except to a limited extent, and it does not cover for example, family or friendly arrangements. At common law, there are different rules regulating the bringing to an end of a tenancy, and an arrangement which amounts only to licence. The housing adviser has to be familiar with all of these provisions.

In this book, we are not concerned to examine housing arrangements in the way that, for example, a sociologist might wish to do, in order to analyse the various different accommodation arrangements that individuals make. We are concerned with housing law. This means that the reader must familiarise himself with the language and terminology of housing law, even to the exclusion of popular terminology. It means that not only must the reader cope with the intrinisic difficulties of the study itself, but must also abandon pre-conceptions and, perhaps, expectations. No matter how familiar a reader may believe himself to be with housing problems in practice, housing law is a wholly separable study and it is necessary to start, as it were, from the very beginning in order to establish a framework in which to examine the details.

This attitude is not adopted by way of preference, but by way of necessity. If it is true to remark that the combinations of arrangements which people will make in order to provide themselves with housing is unlimited, then an examination of the law which is based on that variety of arrangements would also be unlimited. It is necessary, then, to fit the way people live into the law relating to housing, rather than the other way around, even though in many cases the concepts may seem ill-suited or not easily adaptable, *e.g.* in domestic situations, whether of parents and children or of cohabitees.

For a social worker it is, however, a worthwhile exercise. Once the basic material has been learned, it will be easy in the vast majority of cases to identify without difficulty just what sort of accommodation arrangement a person has, how the law will treat it, what his rights, privileges, duties and remedies are, and indeed, how to exercise them. It is only in a minority of cases that it will be problematic to identify the exact nature of an occupier's protection, and in a minority of cases in which it will not be immediately apparent what should be done to assist the occupier or to improve his position. Unfortunately, experience shows that it is in this minority of situations that the social worker will find many of his clients living, as subject to housing insecurity as they are also likely to have gained the least material security generally.

A social worker should be prepared to assist his client on all sorts of topics, including housing. A recent study by Age Concern Greater London, *Housing Advice For The Elderly* observed that many of the elderly turn to their social workers for advice on many subjects of which housing was one of the most common. In any general aid or advice agency, amongst whose clients there will be many who are likely to be the clients of social workers, usually the greatest number of recorded enquiries will be about housing problems.

To discharge his duties to his client properly, the social worker must be sure that the advice he gives is accurate. Inaccurate information can have serious consequences. For example, those tenants who receive the full benefit of Rent Act protection can apply to a Rent Officer to have their rents registered with virtually no undesirable consequences to themselves, even though this means that the landlord will have to accept perhaps a much lower rent than has been agreed. But those tenants who do not have full protection, but only the restricted security offered by the Rent Tribunal, will commonly find that an application for registration of a lower rent results in a retaliatory notice to quit and wholly lawful eviction proceedings (against which there is no defence) at the earliest time that the landlord can make them leave. Whether or not a tenant does have full protection is, therefore, a most important question.

The social worker needs to know what basic rights there are, and how to exercise them. But he should also be aware of when a problem is of sufficient complexity to merit the assistance of a Housing Aid or Law Centre, or of a lawyer in private practice. He should know how to achieve such assistance (Appendix 2) and he should be in a position to explain to a client just what is happening when, as will sometimes happen, a housing problem takes the client into the netherland of the court system (Appendix 1).

The social worker should also be aware that changes in this area of the law take place very frequently indeed. These are not only legislative changes, which are likely to come to the attention of any well-read individual, but also changes brought about by new court decisions, which may be unreported in the popular press. At the present time, the Department of the Environment is conducting a Review of the Rent Acts: it is likely that this will result in a reconsideration of the fair rent system described in Chapter 4. As a result of the decision in *Marchant* v. *Charters*, and that in *Somma* v. *Hazelhurst and Ravelli*, it may well be that there will be a new definition of the distinction between tenant and licensee which has already been referred to and which is described to some extent below and more fully in Chapter 2. It is considered highly probable that if a Conservative government returns to power there will be at the least a new form of letting outside of full Rent Act protection, and, possibly, a wholesale reconsideration of the effects of the Rent Act 1974 which brought furnished lettings into full protection.

Throughout the text, references will be found to be companion volume to this work, *Housing: Repairs and Improvements*, by Tom Hadden. Housing problems rarely exist in isolation. For example, a problem may on the face of it be a financial problem. But the financial difficulties may themselves be attributable to high heating costs and other expenses, the result of damp or otherwise bad housing conditions. Similarly, conditions bad enough to merit a closing order can result in loss of protection (see Chap. 4). The two books have been separated in order to make each more accessible, but both are likely to be of equally common relevance.

In this book, it has not been intended to qualify the reader to advise on every aspect or possible problem arising in the housing situation. The problems and rights of owner-occupiers, for example, are only dealt with briefly, in Chapter 3, as are those which will arise on the breakup of a relationship, considered in Chapter 9. The approach has been both necessarily and deliberately selective. The three objectives which have been considered to be of the greatest importance are:

(a) That the reader should be able to identify what sort of protection an occupier has, and how to take advantage of what the law offers by way of security of tenure, rent control and further financial protection; and

(b) That the reader should be aware of the scope of other possibilities, such as financial assistance through the welfare benefit system, the right to rehousing when homeless, and the laws which may apply when a relationship does break up; and

(c) That the reader should be in a position to make an informed and intelligent contribution when a problem does arise, so that the occupier is not solely dependent upon the quality of the professional advice which is sought.

This last comment bears some elaboration. If it is not

already self-evident that housing law is complex, then it will rapidly become so. It is not only lay occupiers and lay advisers, for example, in advice centres, who are often bewildered by it, but many lawyers, too, are not fully informed about the state of the law. This can be because they are not up-to-date with recent developments, have not been trained to deal with the problems of occupiers, may not even be aware of basic rights and frequently are not aware of many of the finer points which may affect a situation. If a social worker assisting a client through a housing problem does no more than ensure that he is receiving the correct and most appropriate advice, then he will still have made a powerful contribution.

In the rest of this chapter, we shall take a closer look at some of the elements of housing law which have been referred to above, in a slightly different breakdown:

1. *The Common Law*;
2. *Acts of Parliament*;
3. *Landlords*; and
4. *The Courts*.

There are times when a student of this subject can become so bogged down in detail that he loses sight of the overall framework. Modern housing law is about the right of the occupier not to be deprived unreasonably of his home, and only to have to pay a fair or reasonable amount for use of it; the efforts of landlords to let out their accommodation for the greatest profit and yet retain the greatest freedom of disposal of it; and the rule of law through the courts which determines just what the rights and wrongs of a particular situation are and when and to what extent an Act of Parliament affects an arrangement. The subject could be likened to a game of ring-around-rosy, with the tenant in the middle and the politicians, judges and landlords dancing around them. Were it not for the very serious consequences to occupiers, it would be hard to resist this analogy. To pursue it momentarily — the rules of the game are described in the rest of this book, and the two, wholly inconsistent objectives of the major parties are, as stated above:

(i) on the part of the landlords, to retain the greatest freedom of action in the use and disposal of their housing stock; and

(ii) on the part of the tenants, to pay only a socially acceptable rent and not to be evicted unreasonably from their homes.

1. *The Common Law*

The common law of England and Wales is that which is not
contained in Acts of Parliament but which is understood and
accepted to be the basic rules and rights of our society. It is to
be found in ancient textbooks, and in the reports of judicial
decisions made over several centuries. In relation to land, and
therefore, housing, the common law has made many contributions:

At any given point in time, the majority of the population
will be physically in juxtaposition to some piece of land, given
that land includes buildings. This is a fact of life. It also
provides material for legal analysis: what is the relationship
between that individual and the land that he is on? At
common law, there are only four such relationships possible:

(i) A person may own the land that he is on;

(ii) A person may be on land which belongs to another,
without any permission at all. This is known as trespass;

(iii) A person may be on land which belongs to another, and
have permission to be there, without having been granted a
tenancy of the land. This is known as licence; and

(iv) A person may be on land which belongs to another, and
have been granted a tenancy of it. A tenancy is, in effect, a
slice of time in the exclusive use of the land. During the
tenancy, it is the tenant, not the owner (or landlord) who has
possession of the land, and the landlord merely retains ultimate ownership of it. When the time runs out, the use of the
land reverts to the owner, at least in theory, although modern
protective legislation often prevents this happening.

This basic breakdown of occupation is still of paramount
importance in housing law. In particular, an understanding of
the distinction between tenancy and licence is one without
which there can be no comprehension of the subject at all.
Most protective legislation which has been produced in this
century benefits tenants, and most licensees have very little
protection from the law at all.

The most obvious example of licence is that which was given

above: the permission which a child has to be in the house of his parents is a licence, not a tenancy. Similarly, if a person invites a friend to dinner, he cannot be a trespasser, because he has permission, but not for a moment would it be considered that he had become a tenant. The same would be true even if he stayed overnight, or for a few days.

But there are other forms of occupation which are less obviously licences. Hotels do not normally grant tenancies, but grant licences. So do hostels, old people's homes, the permission which an employee sometimes has to live in the same premises as he works is not always tenancy, *e.g.* au pair. There are other occasions when occupation is considered to be by way of licence rather than tenancy, even although the licensee may be paying rent for use of the premises in question.

In every case, however, it is the law, not the parties, which decides what is the relationship between the occupier and the premises in question. If this were not so, then there would be few tenancies in existence at all for, as has already been remarked, most protection is given to tenants rather than licensees, and it is far easier to bring a licence to an end and evict the occupier, than it is to bring a tenancy to an end and get rid of the tenant. It does not even matter if an agreement has been signed stating that the arrangement is that of licence:

> "It does not necessarily follow that a document described as a licence is, merely on that account, to be regarded as amounting only to a licence in law. The whole of the document must be looked at and if, after it has been examined, the right conclusion appears to be that, whatever label has been attached to it, it in fact conferred and imposed on the grantee in substance the rights and obligations of a landlord, then it must be given the appropriate effect, that is to say, it must be treated as a tenancy agreement as distinct from a mere licence ... The important statement of principle is that the relationship is determined by the law, and not by the label the parties choose to put on it, and that it is not necessary to find the document a sham. It is simply a matter of ascertaining the true relationship of the parties ... " (Jenkins, L.J, *Addiscombe Garden Estates Ltd* v. *Crabbe*).

The same principles apply whether or not the arrangement

is in writing. This principle is of overriding importance and, together with another which will be described in 2, below, is one of the two overriding principles which will be referred to as such throughout this book.

The common law has made other contributions. It is a rule of common law that an action for possession in the courts cannot be commenced until any tenancy or licence has actually run out. The law normally requires a landlord to take such an action before evicting an occupier: see Chapter 8. Possession actions are described in outline in Appendix 1.

The common law has over the years built up a code which defines when a notice to quit purporting to bring a tenancy to an end is effective. As regards licences, it is the common law which introduced the requirement that they must be brought to an end by any contractually agreed form and period of notice, or by a reasonable time, whichever is the longer: in other words, that whatever has been agreed between the parties, a person must still have a reasonable time to get out of premises he has been occupying, or, indeed, even just visiting, before he becomes a trespasser.

Even though the common law has been in operation for many hundreds of years, it continues to develop. The courts can even today declare that some rule or other is a rule of common law, or can reinterpret what has hitherto been understood to be the common law. It remains in a state of fluidity, which makes it exceptionally hard to study, especially in comparison to law created by legislation. In studying the common law, the reader must appreciate that what is being studied is a series of principles rather than rules. It is the principles which must be understood, and the facts surrounding the principle are to be read merely as illustrative of it. The basic tenets of the common law as outlined above are examined in detail in Chapter 2 of this book. It is both a difficult and an essential part of the work. Without a comp-prehension of these basic ideas, the remainder of the material in the book may be incorrectly applied.

In addition to these elements of the common law, in Chapter 8 and Appendix 1, we shall encounter further qualities which it has introduced into legal practice. In Chapter 8, we shall consider what an occupier who is being harassed or who has been evicted can do about his situation. Some of this law is statute law, *i.e.* law contained in an Act of Parliament. But one of the steps that such an occupier may take is to go to a county court for assistance. In order to receive assistance from a civil court, it is necessary to show to it that the applicant has what the law calls a "cause of action," that is to say that something is wrong which the law recognises it has authority to deal with. Causes of action can be for breach of contract, or they can be for what is called a "tort," a civil wrong such as assault, nuisance, negligence, trespass, etc. These causes of action have, for the most part, been introduced by the common law.

And what the courts can do about complaints are all remedies which have been devised by the common law: the right to award damages, the right to grant an injunction, the right to declare what is the correct status of the parties in relation to, *e.g.* some premises, and so on. These too, however, have also been affected in part by legislation.

It is worth bearing in mind from the outset the distinction between a civil and a criminal action. A civil action governs relationships between individuals, and gives one individual the right to sue another. A criminal action will arise when one person has done something which the law considers to be an offence against society as a whole and which renders the accused liable to be prosecuted, usually not by the victim but by one of the public bodies charged with prosecution duties. In relation to housing, there are a number of criminal offences, although these have all been created by statute, rather than by the common law.

2. *Acts of Parliament*

Acts of Parliament are the second, and equally important, source of law. They are the source of the protective legislation which prevents landlords charging excessive rents and evicting occupiers arbitrarily. Protective legislation creates both civil rights and criminal offences. For example, there are criminal offences in relation to harassment and illegal eviction, described in Chapter 8; through other chapters of this book, there will be found references to criminal offences concerning the overcharging of rents, asking for premiums (also known as key money) before people are allowed into premises, failing to provide rent books and failing to tell a tenant the name and address of a landlord.

The main body of protective legislation has already been referred to; the Rent Acts. The Rent Act is aimed primarily at tenants rather than licensees. It gives those tenants who gain the full benefit of the Acts the right to apply to a Rent Officer for registration of a fair rent, and to remain in occupation of premises even after a tenancy has been brought to an end. Acts of Parliament and the common law coexist, although not always with much harmony. When a person is granted a tenancy of premises, he becomes the contractual (common law) tenant of them; if he afterwards is protected by the Rent Acts, he becomes what is called the statutory tenant of them. Through both the contractual and the statutory tenancies, both common law terms of occupation and statutory regulation can affect the position of the parties.

It has already been said that not all tenants are fully protected. There are tenants of resident landlords who, in the main, are not. There are tenants of local authorities and housing associations who are also excluded from the Act, in whole or part. Some protection applies to some of those who have no tenancy in premises, but only a contractual licence. The levels of statutory protection apply to the common law concepts of occupation. There are three levels of protection which occupiers may take advantage of:

(i) *Full security*

This is the right to remain indefinitely in premises, until a landlord establishes one of the legislative "grounds for possession" with which to secure a court order for possession. There is also a right to have a fair rent registered for the tenancy which limits the amount a landlord can charge. Those who have full security are protected tenants and they and their rights are described in Chapter 4.

(ii) *Restricted security*

This is the right to apply to the Rent Tribunal for registration of a reasonable rent and for limited security of tenure.

This class of protection affects some tenants, mostly those with resident landlords, and even some contractual licensees, *e.g.* some hostel dwellers. The jurisdiction and powers of the Rent Tribunal are described in Chapter 5.

(iii) *Basic security*

Whether or not an occupier falls within full or restricted security, most occupiers are entitled to remain in occupation of premises until such time as a court (which will usually be the county court) makes an order for possession which compels them to leave and authorises the court bailiff to evict the occupier. Occupiers who do not fall within full or restricted security are not without any rights at all. They include the tenants of the public authorities. They, and their rights, are described in Chapter 6, although the whole subject of eviction without a court order (*i.e.* illegal eviction) is considered, together with the problem of harassment, in Chapter 8.

What sort of protection an occupier has is, again, a matter of law, not a matter of private arrangement between the parties. There is a housing shortage. Would-be occupiers will agree to almost any terms in order to get a roof over their heads. They will agree to pay rents they cannot afford, and to stay for only short periods, although they are looking for permanent homes. The legislation is there to protect them from exploitation. If landlords could simply compel occupiers to sign agreements that waived their rights under the Rent Act and other protective legislation, then the rent Acts would rarely if ever have any effect at all. Nor can a landlord avoid the effects of protective legislation by dressing up an arrangement which falls within one level of protection, so as to look as if it falls within another. This produces the second of the overriding principles of which that concerning tenancy or licence was the first:

> "It has been said before, and it must be said again, that in the consideration of questions arising under the Rent Acts, the court must look at the substance and reality of a transaction, not its form ... " (Viscount Simonds, *Elmdene Estates* v. *White.*)

In an earlier case, *Samrose Properties Ltd.* v. *Gibbard,*

Lord Evershed, MR, said that a court must always ask itself:
" ... whether the transaction, viewed as a whole and
according to the substance of it, is in truth one which ... is
on that side of the line which frees the premises from the
impact of the Acts, or whether, so regarded, the transaction
is one which is of the mischief which the Acts were designed
to avoid."

The extent of Rent Act protection can and does change.
Different political parties have different views as to just how
much the state ought to intervene in housing arrangements,
and how much should be left to traditional, free enterprise
principles of proprietorship. One tradition which both major
political parties share, however, is that those who have full
protection at a time when new legislation is contemplated
should not be deprived of it, *i.e.* that any new legislation
should affect only new lettings.

This produces additional legal complexities as frequently as
new Rent Act legislation comes into force. For example, the
1974 Rent Act granted to furnished tenants the same extent of
protection that had hitherto been enjoyed by unfurnished
tenants, *i.e.* full security. Before the date when that Act came
into operation (August 14, 1974, a date which will be referred
to frequently throughout this book) furnished tenants had
restricted security only. But at the same time, a new class of
occupier was defined, the tenant with a resident landlord.
Tenants with resident landlords have restricted security only.
But some tenants with resident landlords were tenants of their
premises before August 14, 1974, and many of them were fully
protected at that date, because the earlier test was that of furnished or unfurnished, irrespective of whether or not there was
a resident landlord. These tenants could not be deprived of
protection. Provision has been made, therefore, to define
when a pre-1974 Rent Act tenant is fully protected and when
only with restricted security. Nor for a moment should it be
thought that the question of whether a tenancy was furnished
or not is one that is easy to answer: it depends not on the simple
provision of furniture, but on the value of the furniture
compared to the rent. This problem will still be encountered,
because of these transitional provisions.

Acts of Parliament make a further, rather dubious

contribution to housing law, through the quality of the draughtsmanship. Rent Acts have almost always been passed under great pressure: from opposition, and because of the social consequences that follow the announcement of intended legislation, which is that the supply of accommodation invariably dries up until the legal position becomes clear once more. There are also frequently evictions, as preceded the Rent Act 1974, as landlords scramble to empty their properties while they are still legally entitled to do so. In the event, hurried legislation is always badly draughted. This means that there is considerable scope for reinterpretation in the courts, possibly loopholes and unconsidered possibilities and, most of all, an unacceptable level of uncertainty amongst those who must live subject to these Acts. In many of the major court decisions on the Acts, the judges have commented on the appalling quality of Rent Act authorship.

3. *The Landlords*

The resentment of landlords towards protective legislation has already been indicated. As a body, landlords do not welcome state intervention in what was traditionally a free enterprise business. During the last century, there was still some tradition alive amongst landlords that a good tenant, who would look after a property, was worth more than the largest amount of immediately available profit. This tradition has long since disappeared. The fact that it may once have been true does not, of course, answer questions about the propriety of leaving in private hands the control of so essential a resource as housing; but these issues are, however, outside the scope of this book.

Certainly, this tradition had expired by the time the protective legislation described in this book came into force. It was bad landlordism which provoked the public health legislation which is the subject of the companion volume, *Housing: Repairs and Improvements*. It was bad landlordism which provoked rent control, and security of tenure. It was bad landlordism which made necessary the morass of additional protective measures which will be encountered in this book, all of them designed to avert the worst of landlordism.

The history of privately rented accommodation in this

century is a history of a pitched battle fought over the conflicting objectives described in the introductory part of this chapter: landlords seeking maximum freedom to speculate and dispose of property at will; tenants seeking maximum housing use of the stock retained in the private sector. It is a battle which has been fought in the courts, in the streets into which tenants have been evicted, in Parliament and in the stop-start supply of accommodation within the sector.

For an example of how this has worked, one may look at the development of furnished accommodation, which has already been referred to in outline. In 1915, when the first Rent Act was passed, working class occupation was in unfurnished premises. Furnished property was a luxury. When one reads the literature of the nineteenth century, Dickens or Eliot, for example, one reads of families who moved up in the world into furnished accommodation and who, when they fell on hard times, had to cast around amongst relatives and charitable friends or institutions for basic life support. Walking around, London for example, one can still see smart, bronze plates outside terraced houses announcing *Furnished Chambers to Let*. Furnished accommodation was often what people, usually well-off, took when they were spending a period of time away from their own, normal homes. In traditional English modes of housing, furniture was a luxury provided to the wealthy and never intended to be a part of that which was provided to, or imposed upon, the majority of tenants. For these reasons, furnished lettings were exempt from the early Rent Acts.

This description of the use of furnished accommodation would come as a surprise to those who, in the fifties, sixties and early seventies, had no choice but to accept furnished accommodation as their permanent homes. What is more, the furniture provided could not be called, by any stretch of the imagination, luxurious. For what had happened was this: the landlords saw that they could retain control over rents and occupation of furnished property by letting it furnished and so, regardless of the imposition upon the lives of tenants, would only let with furniture. In 1946, this trait had grown to such an extent that furnished tenants were given restricted security. But this proved so ineffectual that in 1974, they were brought into full protection.

This has not brought an end to the wiles of landlords seeking to evade protection. Readers who are or have recently been students may have attempted to find accommodation to live in while at college and away from home. They will be familiar with advertisements for "holiday lettings" offered in places like Brixton, North Kensington, Islington or Hammersmith, areas of London, none of which are famous for their contribution to the tourist industry. Or else, they may have found that the arrangement required the occupier to accept from his landlord what he termed "board"; not the full board, or even generous breakfast or supper known to the commercial traveller in a Brighton boarding-house, but instead, a small, cellophane covered, plastic tray consisting of half-a-dozen individual-sized packets of cereal, some long-life milk and, perhaps, six or seven tea bags. A variation on this theme is "board" which consists of a weekly delivery of groceries by the landlord who not only charges an exorbitant price for the food but is also claiming a rent far beyond the reaches of registration.

Yet again, occupiers may have been required to accept what the landlord has termed "attendances"; the services of a resident housekeeper who, allegedly, comes into a room or flat each day to clean it, even though the occupier would far rather save the money he has to pay and do the cleaning himself. Or else the landlord may have compelled the occupier to sign a document which in all other respects resembles a tenancy agreement but which describes itself as a "licence."

The most common recent evasive phenomenon is that of the non-exclusive occupation agreement. This is an extraordinary arrangement under which a series of would-be occupiers, in all respects a group of joint tenants, are required to sign individual and separate agreement with the landlord. These agreements purport to grant the occupier the right to live in particular premises, but in no particular part of them, in common with such others, sometimes including the landlord, as the landlord may select. This particular device is designed to destroy all the elements of protection at one fell swoop: exclusive possession, without which there can be no tenancy, joint tenancy, exclusive occupation even of single rooms within, for example a flat, joint licence within restricted security.

All these arrangements are examples of what landlords may offer with one intent and only one intent in mind: that is to say, the landlord is seeking to evade the effects of protection: rent control and security of tenure. In some cases, he may be successful; in others, the courts, applying the two over-riding principles described above, will fling the arrangement out and use their powers to declare the true nature of the arrangement. In all of them, the occupier will be subject to doubt and uncertainty, and may, pending court action, be obliged to pay an unconscionably high rent. Further-more he will in every case have to rely on the interpreta-tion of the courts for any protection or security at all.

4. *The Courts*

It is the courts which are the final arbiters. The courts are custodians of the common law and they alone have the power to decide what it actually says or means, or how it applies to any given situation. It is the courts which interpret Acts of Parliament and decide just what Parliament intended or, if you like, where the limits of protection lie. It is the courts who will confront the ingenious efforts of particular landlords and decide whether or not he has been successful in his quest for the unprotected letting.

The courts operate in an hierarchic structure. The highest court of the land is the House of Lords. Beneath that, there is the Divisional Court, charged with supervision of administra-tive bodies, such as tribunals and committees, and the activi-ties of the public authorities, and the Court of Appeal (Civil Division) to which all appeals, whether from the High Court or the county court will lie. In addition, there is the Court of Appeal (Criminal Division) to which appeals from the Crown Court are taken. Beneath these courts, there is the High Court and the Crown Court: the latter dealing with serious criminal charges, the former with civil claims involving fairly high amounts of money or values. Neither of these two latter courts will have much to do with the law described in this book. The lowest courts of all are the magistrates' courts and the county court. The latter will hear all civil matters at first instance; the

former will be the first court to which a criminal charge will go
to be heard.

The higher courts are the most influential, because their
decisions are customarily reported and their views on how law
is to be understood or applied bind the lower courts, that is to
say they are bound to follow their decisions. The lower courts
are, however, more important to most individual occupiers as
it is comparatively rare for an appeal to be taken from a
decision of the county or magistrates' court. The county court
is the forum in which most housing rights will be finally
decided.

Reference has already been made to the scope left to the
courts to reinterpret the Rent Acts. For example, the Rent Act
makes provision for subtenants. But the courts have decided
that these provisions only apply where both tenant and subtenant are within full security. Different provisions apply
where either tenant or subtenant is outside of full security, and
these alternative provisions are much less satisfactory from the
occupier's point of view than would be the provisions made by
the Act.

The major capacity for reinterpretation that the courts have
is their authority to interpret the rules of the common law. By
reinterpreting the basic distinction between tenancy and
licence, they can affect the degree of protection which an
occupier enjoys. In one case, *Marcroft Waggons Ltd.* v. *Smith*,
Lord Denning stated quite baldly that before the Rent Acts
had come into operation, he would have considered the
occupation of the woman in question to be by way of tenancy.
As, however, this would mean that she would become fully
protected he was quite prepared to view her occupation as
being by way óf licence which resulted, in that cases, in the loss
of any protection at all. His view was that the courts could
reinterpret the common law in the light of legislation, even
although the legislation would itself be based on the earlier
interpretation of the common law.

The same judge adopted a similar approach in the recent
case of *Marchant* v. *Charters*, in which occupation of a bedsitting-room was in issue. Was this tenancy or licence? There
was nothing on the facts to distinguish the letting from a
"normal" bedsitting-room arrangement, which had hitherto

been considered as constituting tenancy. But Lord Denning found that in this case, the occupier was only a licensee. This he did because the Rent Act 1974 had altered the position of furnished tenants, but not that of furnished licensees. In short, the question was again that of protected or unprotected, and he decided against protection.

On occasion, Parliament will legislate so as to overturn a decision of the courts. This they did after a decision in which it was held that a letting of a single room, even by way of tenancy, could not be protected if the tenant shared any living accommodation, *e.g.* a kitchen, with his landlord or any-one else. Parliament legislated so as to give those who shared with their landlords restricted security, and those who shared with other tenants full security.

The attitude of the courts is one that many see as having been hostile to the idea of protection itself: see, for example the Legal Action Group *Submissions To The Department Of The Environment Review Of The Rent Acts*. It would be dis-ingenuous not to accept that the courts, and in particular the Court of Appeal, have reacted with antipathy to the whole body of protective legislation under consideration in this book. The Rent Acts have interfered extensively with the common law position and, more importantly, with the free trade, private enterprise approach to housing with which the courts are both more familiar and more at home. For an examination of the courts' attitudes to housing, and other protective legis-lation, see *The Politics of the Judiciary*, John Griffiths, (Fontana Books) which is essential reading for anyone seeking to do more than learn simply what the law says, but who wants also to understand how it is likely to be applied in the courts.

2 The Classes of Occupation

At common law, there are only four ways in which a person can come to use premises as a residence:
1. *Owner-occupation*;
2. *Trespass*;
3. *Licence*; and
4. *Tenancy*.

In addition, however, there are combinations of circumstances, some of which must be considered:
5. *Tied accommodation*;
6. *Subtenants*;
7. *Joint tenants*;
8. *Tenants of mortgagers*;
9. *Assignees*; and
10. *Change of landlord*.

1. *Owner-Occupation*

A person who owns the freehold of the house in which he lives, untrammelled by any mortgage, is, of course, the principal "model" for owner-occupation. Such a person has the fullest rights of occupation and protection of all. The right to occupy the house can only be interfered with in very limited sets of circumstances. For example, if a local authority purchases the house compulsorily, perhaps for some new development; or else, if the property falls into considerable disrepair, the local authority might put a closing order or demolition order on the house as a result of which it will become illegal to live in it. Another way in which such an owner-occupier might lose the right of occupation is if he goes into bankruptcy and the trustee in bankruptcy forces its sale. All of these incidents are outside the scope of this book: closing and demolition orders, and clearance by a local authority, are dealt with in the companion volume, *Housing: Repairs and Improvements*. We shall consider one further way in which a freehold owner might come to lose the right to occupy his home, and that is as a result of a court order made in the course of a domestic break-up. This is dealt with in Chapter 9.

Many people who have a freehold interest in their homes, however, do so under mortgage. A mortgage is a loan against the security of property, *i.e.* a house or a flat. The money is usually borrowed in order to buy the property, although sometimes it may be needed for carrying out repairs or improvements. Sometimes, people raise money by way of mortgage simply because they are in other financial difficulties. This should only be done as a last resort. If a person falls into arrears with his mortgage repayments, the mortgage company may evict the occupier: see Chapter 3.

The term owner-occupier is also used, somewhat artificially, to describe those who do not have a freehold interest in their homes, but who have a leasehold interest. A freehold interest is one which is unlimited in time: there is no "superior" interest or landlord who will reclaim it at any point in the future. A leasehold interest is one in which there is one such superior interest, a landlord to whom, is paid a small, annual ground rent and who, in theory at least, is entitled to reclaim the property at the end of the lease. A leasehold interest is for a period of more than 21 years. In practice, on the termination of the lease, the occupier has rights of protection similar to those enjoyed by other tenants and, in some circumstances, a leasehold occupier may have the very considerably greater protection afforded by a right to compel the landlord to sell to him the freehold. These rights will be considered in Chapter 3.

Leasehold interests may be held under mortgage, although it will usually not be possible to obtain a mortgage on a leasehold property unless there is at least 30 years to run on the lease. This is because mortgage companies want to have security for their loan, and must calculate what they can recover by resale of the property if the occupier falls into arrears on the mortgage at any given point in time. If the occupier falls into arrears in the last few years, the mortgage company will not have much to resell: but, then, there will not be much of a debt outstanding on the property because so much will already have been paid off. If the occupier falls into arrears soon after the mortgage is granted, there will be adequate time left on the lease for the mortgage company to recoup its loan.

Many people do not purchase a leasehold interest from the freeholder. They take it, instead, from an existing leaseholder, commonly the existing occupier who is selling his interest. During the course of such a transaction, the freeholder will have little or nothing to do with the arrangements, save perhaps to give his consent to them. Where a would-be occupier under leasehold purchases from an outgoing lease-holder, the transaction is called an assignment, but is in all other respects much like a straightforward purchase. It does not matter that there may be less than 21 years to run on the lease: the incoming occupier will still be termed an owner-occupier. It is the length of the interest itself, *i.e.* the lease, not the length of occupation which determines whether or not a person has a leasehold interest which qualifies as owner-occupation. For example, a weekly tenant who had lived in premises for more than 21 years would not thereby become an owner-occupier.

2. *Trespass*

From those with the greatest rights of occupation, to those with the least. A trespasser is one who occupies premises without any permission at all to do so. Such permission may be given by anyone in a position to grant the authority. For example, an owner may obviously give permission to occupy property, but so may his agent, or a director of a company which owns property, or even someone who is himself no more than a tenant. A tenant is in a position to give permission because so long as his tenancy lasts, it is the tenant, rather than the land-lord or the owner, who has possession of the premises. It follows, therefore, that an owner or a landlord could not give someone else permission to occupy premises if he had already let them to a tenant.

Because of the housing shortages which exist in most areas of the country, trespass is far from uncommon. Many are forced to trespass simply in order to find somewhere to live. This is the phenomenon, by no means as recent as the popular press would lead one to believe, of squatting. Of course, there could not be so much squatting as there has been in recent years were it not for the extraordinary amount of property which has been kept vacant during the housing shortages. There may be many reasons why property is kept vacant; it may be because someone is abroad or away for a time, it may be because the property is subject to negotiations, between private occupiers or between property speculators, or simply withheld from the market until a favourable time to sell, or it may be because it is unfit for occupation, or it may be because there are plans to redevelop or renew the properties at some time in the future and they have been emptied prematurely.

In fact, the squatting movement has created so much pressure upon public authorities, and those who are in some way answerable to the public for use of their properties, that many local authorities and housing associations now consent to properties being "squatted" for some specific time, or else until they are ready to be redeveloped. There is little popular distinction between those who squat without permission, and those who use short-life property with permission. But there is considerable difference in law: those without permission are trespassers, those who have permission are licensees. The term squatter is not one which it is appropriate to use in discussions of housing law, although in one case in which it was used (*McPhail* v. *Persons Unknown*) the description given to squatting was consistent with trespass, rather than licence. This does not mean that all squatters are trespassers, but simply that if the term is to be used in law, it must be confined to those who squat without permission. So far as possible, therefore, for the avoidance of confusion, the term squatter will not be used further in this book.

Because of the growth of squatting, and, largely, because of unfounded fears that squatters would take over individuals' homes while they are away on holiday, legislation has recently been introduced to deal with the situation. This is contained in the Criminal Law Act 1977 and will be considered further in Chapter 6.

3. *Licence*

We have already referred to one, common example of licence: a person living in property which is either owned or rented by a member of his family, *e.g.* a parent, is a licensee of that person. Similarly, a cohabitee is a licensee of his partner, if it is the partner who owns or is the tenant of the accommodation in which they live. Technically, if one spouse is the owner or tenant of the matrimonial home, the other spouse is only his licensee, but it has been held that, as a matter of practice and as a matter of good taste, it is inappropriate to consider one spouse as the licensee of another (*National Provincial Bank Ltd.* v. *Ainsworth*) and the position of both spouses and cohabitees will be considered in the context of breakup of the relationship in Chapter 9.

The term "licence" means no more than "permission," whether used in connection with housing, or with driving a car, or selling alcohol. In the housing context, it is used to describe one who is not a trespasser (because he has permission to occupy) but who is neither an owner-occupier, nor a tenant. Were it not for this class of occupation, there would be no term appropriate for such people as family, friends or casual guests.

Some people are quite obviously no more than licensees of another. Common sense dictates that a friend who comes to stay for a while is not to be considered a tenant of the host, while at the same time he cannot be a trespasser because, of course, he is there by the host's invitation. This position does not change simply because, for example, the guest is invited to stay for several weeks and even agrees to pay some sort of contribution towards the housekeeping expenses, or indeed, a fixed sum of rent. It will never have been intended that the friend should become a tenant and the law will not treat him as such. It is quite common for a person to have such a sharer living with him and he will not be considered a tenant. This is considered further at 7, below.

There are other arrangements, however, where it is less immediately obvious whether a person is to be considered a licensee or a tenant. If someone goes to stay in a hotel for a few days, for example, it would not be considered that he had become a tenant of the hotel. But what if he made his home over a number of years in the hotel? There are many who live for considerable periods of time in hotels, (more commonly cheaper, long-stay hotels) who have nowhere else to live and who regard the hotel as a home. In *Luganda* v. *Service Hotels Ltd.* the Court of Appeal considered that, nonetheless, such an occupier was only a licensee and did not become a tenant.

In the same way, the occupier of a hostel is usually considered a mere licensee: *e.g.* a YWCA hostel, as in *R* v. *South Middlesex Rent Tribunal, ex parte Beswick*, or one of the many hostels which exist not primarily to provide housing for people, but principally to rehabilitate those who have had some sort of difficulty, such as drug addicts, mental patients, prisoners, and only secondarily, in order to achieve the rehabilitative effect, provide housing for some period or other: *Trustees of the Alcoholic Recovery Project* v. *Farrell*. The distinction which may be drawn between hostels and houses of bedsitting-rooms is that in the hostel there is normally a resident housekeeper, and the occupier is bound to obey rules and regulations which interfere far more than normal housing management rules do with the occupier's way of life.

Another example of a similar sort of situation is provided by the case of *Abbeyfield (Harpenden) Society Ltd.* v. *Woods*. In this case, the society ran an old people's home, consisting of single rooms for which the old people paid a weekly rent. The project could only exist satisfactorily so long as each of the occupiers was self-sufficient. Once an elderly person required constant care and attention, it was no longer possible for him to go on living there. There were not the facilities for the provision of such assistance and, clearly, in a house containing nothing but the elderly, the consequences could be disastrous. In the event, it was held that the occupier was only a licensee, not a tenant.

Acts of kindness or generosity are deemed not to be the acts from which tenancies spring. In *Booker* v. *Palmer*, a city family were provided with accommodation in the country during the war. They later suggested that they had become tenants of the property but the Court of Appeal applied what it termed a "golden rule" of interpretation of such matters. This is that the courts will not impute intention to enter into the sort of legal intention implied by tenancy where the spirit of the arrangement is family or friendly.

This attitude found some extension in the case of *Marcroft Waggons Ltd.* v. *Smith*, which was referred to in Chapter 1. In that case, a woman had lived with her parents in a cottage for 50 years. Her father was the original tenant, and on his death, his wife was entitled by the law then in force to "succeed" to the tenancy. However, only one such "succession" was then permitted (unlike the position now, see Chapter 4) and on the death of her mother, the daughter faced eviction. She asked for the tenancy to be granted to her but the landlords refused. They permitted her to remain on in occupation, however, in order to find somewhere else to live, and continued to charge her the same weekly rent as her mother had been paying. It was in this case that Lord Denning held that prior to the introduction of the Rent Acts, the daughter would have been deemed to have become the tenant of the landlords, on the principles later stated in *Addiscombe Garden Estates Ltd.* v. *Crabbe*, p. 10, but that in view of the implications of such a finding, *i.e.* that she would enjoy the full force of Rent Act protection, he considered that they should interpret the arrangement as no more than licence. The court emphasised that this could only be the result where the would-be tenant was already in occupation of the premises at the time the arrangement was made; if an arrangement on those lines was offered to someone not living in the premises, this would still constitute tenancy. Nor will it be a licence in every case where an occupier is allowed to stay on after the tenant leaves: it is a question of fact and intention every time.

In *Marchant* v. *Charters*, also referred to in Chapter 1, there was a house of bedsitting rooms: each of the occupiers had cooking facilities and equipment in his own room, the rooms were furnished and the occupiers lived wholly separate lives, that is to say there were no communal facilities. The house was expressed to be let, and was actually let "to single men only," and there was a resident housekeeper with whom an arrangement could be made for the provision of evening meals, although this was not an obligatory part of the accommodation arrangement and was not something agreed to by the occupier in question. None of these circumstances would individually cause the arrangement to be considered only a licence. Indeed, many would have thought that even taken together there was nothing to distinguish the arrangement from a conventional bedsitting-room letting; such lettings have always been considered to constitute tenancies, rather than licences. Nonetheless, it was held that, in the individual circumstances of the case, the occupier was no more than a licensee.

In all of these cases, the true test is what was intended by the parties. The cases above are only illustrative of circumstances in which the intention necessary for tenancy was found to be lacking. This does not mean what was intended by one party or the other, for otherwise in every case a landlord would indicate intention only to let on licence, and there would be few tenancies for the Rent Acts to apply to at all. The question of intention is one determined by the law, on examination of the arrangement as a whole, and in particular any terms of it, subject to those two overriding principles described in Chapter 1. The sorts of term from which the courts will interpret intention to create tenancy are illustrated by these:

(i) An agreement in which the occupier is to be liable for repairs, insuring the premises or decorating is likely to be one which the courts will describe as tenancy, for they are such extensive obligations that one would not normally anticipate an occupier with the reduced, or limited, interest of licence only being obliged to take them on.

(ii) An agreement which expressly prohibits the occupier from subletting or assigning the right of occupation will normally be considered a tenancy, for it is not possible to assign or sublet a licence and so, by implication, the true nature of the arrangement is revealed as tenancy.

Indeed, one may deduce from the cases that where a landlord offers a written agreement stating that the arrangement is licence only, such a degree of premeditation is implied that the courts will be reluctant to believe that only a licence was truly intended. The converse is not true: oral tenancy agreements are a long-established and standard form of letting by way of tenancy in this country.

In every case, one should ask whether the arrangement is the normal arrangement by which one person comes to occupy the premises of another for use as a home, customarily paying rent in money for the right. If it is, then this is tenancy, and it is the cornerstone of the business of landlordism itself. Once the occupier is paying for the accommodation, then there must be some overriding reason, such as those illustrated above, which reduces the occupation to that of licence, by way of destroying intention to create tenancy. The absence of a rent book will not be sufficient to achieve this. Strictly, it is not necessary to pay rent in order to establish that there is a tenancy, but the courts tend to look sceptically in this day and age at any arrangement purporting to be tenancy under which no rent is paid (*Heslop* v. *Burns*) and will only be prepared to do so if they can find some other consideration.

A person who is a trespasser but who is subsequently given permission, not amounting to tenancy, to remain on the premises becomes a licensee. A person whose licence is brought to an end becomes, technically, a trespasser. However, most of the recent laws relating to trespass (brought in to deal with squatting) do not affect those who entered as licensees but subsequently became trespassers. Some licensees are entitled to refer their contracts to the Rent Tribunal which has power to register a reasonable rent for the premises, and which also has power to defer a notice to leave premises occupied under licence. This is considered in greater detail in Chapter 5.

Licensees may be termed "bare licensees," or may be termed "contractual licensees." One who is, by arrangement, paying a fixed sum of money for the right of occupation will be a contractual licensee. A friend, member of the family, or cohabitee, even although he may be paying some amount by way of contribution to household expenses, will normally be considered a bare licensee. The distinction may not be wholly irrelevant when the question of bringing a licence to an end arises. So long as the licence remains in existence, the licensee not only commits no offence by remaining on premises but, indeed, cannot be turned off them without the person who does so himself committing an offence: see Chapter 8. Once the licence comes to an end, however, which may include a period of extension granted by the Rent Tribunal, the person who is immediately entitled to possession of the premises in question, which may be the owner of the premises, or may be a landlord, or, indeed, may even be only a tenant of the premises, can reclaim possession from the former licensee. In some circumstances, it is necessary to obtain a court order before evicting the former licensee, and an offence is committed if this is not done. In other circumstances, it may not be necessary to obtain a court order. But unless the licence has been duly brought to an end, the person who seeks possession is not entitled to re-claim it, with or without court proceedings.

There are a few arrangements which may be described as "fixed term" licences. That is to say, the period for which the right of occupation has been granted is fixed in advance. These arrangements require no notice to be given to bring them to an end because, in effect, the notice has been given at the outset of the arrangement. Most licences, however, are not for a fixed period but exist from week to week, even day to day, or perhaps as much as from month to month. In such cases, it is necessary to give notice in order to bring the arrangement to an end. It may be that some agreement about either the length or form of notice has been reached in the course of arranging the licence in the first place: *e.g.* one month's notice in writing. This is not a necessary element of a licence. If there is such an agreement, it would indicate that the licence was a contractual, not a bare licence. If there is such an agreement in force, then the licence cannot be determined except in accordance with it, for the law will not support a breach of contract.

Whether or not there is such agreement, however, the law implies into every licence, whether bare or contractual, a term that it will not be brought to an end without reasonable notice being given. This means that a licence agreement which contractually provided for, *e.g.* one day's notice would not be brought to an end in one day, unless the law considered one day a reasonable time.

What is a reasonable time is a question of fact. It will depend upon many circumstances: how long the licensee has been in occupation, how much furniture or property he has in the premises, how much family, what alternative arrangements have been or could be made, even the time of day or night could affect it. In addition, behaviour may affect what the law views as a reasonable time for determination of a licence. A violent licensee will not be given much time at all, *e.g.* a violent man who is cohabiting with the woman who is tenant or owner-occupier cannot expect a matter of weeks in which to leave, even if he has lived in the property for years. Where the arrangement is close to tenancy, however, such as in a hostel or long-stay hotel, the courts will be inclined to view four weeks as a reasonable time, by analogy with that which is required for all residential tenants: see p. 34. The courts will never consider an indefinite or infinite period a reasonable time, no matter how hard it is to find alternative accommodation. Indeed, they will rarely exceed four weeks.

The rule may be shortly stated in this way: a licensee is entitled to a reasonable period of notice *or* a contractually agreed period of notice, whichever is the *longer*. Most occupiers will take court proceedings against a former licensee in order to secure his departure, because the risk of committing a criminal offence when evicting without a court order is very high indeed: see Chapter 8. Court proceedings may be brought in the normal way, see Appendix 1, or by a special, speedy form of procedure originally intended for trespassers, but also applicable to licensees. This is a short application to the court known as Order 26, in the county court, and Order 113 in the High Court. If these speedy proceedings are used, then the person seeking to evict the former licensee must establish that the licence came to an end *before* the application was issued at the court. If normal proceedings are used, it is enough to show that the licence has expired by the time of the court hearing.

4. *Tenancy*

This is the normal arrangement by which one person comes to occupy premises which are owned by another. It is, of course, customarily granted in exchange for a monetary payment, rent. It has been said that this is not an essential element of tenancy but, except in the context of service tenancy (see 5 below), it is so likely that an arrangement under which no rent is paid will be considered a mere licence that it will not be considered further here.

There are two common forms of tenancy: periodic tenancies and fixed term tenancies. A periodic tenancy is one which is granted to run from period to period, *e.g.* week to week or month to month. It can only be brought to an end by service of a valid notice to quit. A fixed term tenancy is one which is granted for a specific period of time, *e.g.* three months, six months or a year, and this normally comes to an end simply because the time runs out. Neither sort of tenancy needs to be in writing, except for fixed term tenancies in excess of three years. A landlord under a *weekly* tenancy (but no other) is obliged to provide a rent book, and commits a criminal offence if he does not do so. Under section 121, of the Housing Act 1974, *any* tenant can ask, in writing, the person who last received rent under the tenancy, what the full name and address of the landlord is. If the person to whom the demand is made fails to reply, also in writing, within 21 days, he also commits an offence. This may be important information if, for example, the tenant wants to commence court proceedings against an unknown landlord and cannot do so without first establishing his identity. Both of these offences should be reported to the Tenancy Relations or Harassment Officer: see Chapter 8.

As well as the two ways mentioned above, there are two other common ways of bringing a tenancy to an end. One is by way of surrender. It occurs, commonly, when a tenant wants to leave accommodation before the end of a fixed term. Strictly, a surrender happens by drawing up a formal declaration of surrender. However, it can also happen by operation of law, if the tenant performs some unequivocal act of surrender, such as returning the keys to the landlord, or such as removing from the premises all signs of occupation, including furniture, belongings and any family or friends who were living with him, and the landlord accepts these acts as acts of surrender. The landlord is not obliged to do so and can continue to consider the tenant liable for rent and other tenant's responsibilities in the premises. Most landlords, however, welcome any departure of a tenant and seize upon often inadequate acts of surrender as a sign that the tenant has departed. Naturally, this does not constitute surrender: there has to be full and unequivocal mutuality about the surrender.

The other common way of bringing a tenancy to an end, and one that is also normally only used in connection with fixed term tenancies, is forfeiture. In order for there to be a forfeiture, there must be a provision in the agreement that forfeiture can occur. Commonly, forfeiture is something which the landlord can claim to have occurred automatically once rent has been in arrears for a stated period of time, *e.g.* 14 days. It can also be a part of an agreement that forfeiture will occur if some other breach of the tenancy takes place. When there is a forfeiture in this way, the landlord claims to "re-enter" the premises, but cannot in practice do this because of the rules governing eviction of tenants. A court has power to order "relief" from forfeiture, if the breach of the tenancy has been remedied, *e.g.* arrears of rent have been paid off. Relief effectively reinstates the tenancy.

Neither of these latter two ways of bringing a tenancy to an end are commonly used in connection with periodic tenancies because of the comparative ease with which these can be determined by notice to quit. Notice to quit a tenancy is a formal and technical document, to which old common law rules apply, as well as modern regulations introduced by legislation. Notice to quit can be given by either landlord or tenant, although it is uncommon for a tenant to give notice to quit with sufficient degree of accuracy for it to qualify as such. An invalid notice to quit may be treated as valid by the party who receives it, at least insofar as the technicalities of the common law are concerned, and a landlord who receives an invalid notice from the tenant may treat this as a surrender. If the tenant subsequently changes his mind about departing, whether after notice to quit or surrender, the landlord will still have to take court proceedings to evict him and might not be able to do so.

All notices to quit residential tenancies must be in writing, must be of a *minimum* length of four weeks (*Protection From Eviction Act, 1977, s. 5*) and must expire on either the last day or the first day of a period of the tenancy. This last condition is derived from the common law, as is the provision that the notice must also be of at least one full period's length of tenancy, so that a four week notice to quit a monthly tenancy would not be valid, as a month is longer than four weeks. However, only six months' notice is required to terminate a yearly periodic tenancy. A notice to quit which is of insufficient length will not become valid at a later, correct time, but will be wholly invalid. This is unlike a notice bringing a licence to an end, since even if the notice gave insufficient time, it may nonetheless, become valid at a later point in time. Because of this need for accuracy, many notices to quit, from landlords to tenants, add a saving clause, which will read something like this: " ... on the 13th day of December 1977 or at the end of the period of your tenancy expiring next four weeks after service of this notice upon you." Such a saving clause is wholly valid and if December 13, 1977 was neither the first nor the last day of a period of the tenancy, the notice to quit would take effect on the next of those two possible days, four weeks after service. The rent day is normally the first day of the tenancy, in the absence of evidence that it is another day.

Service of a notice to quit has to be personal. Most service is effected by post, although some service is carried out by leaving it at the premises. It is not validly served until the tenant himself receives it. A notice to quit must identify the premises the subject of the tenancy, so that a notice given for the wrong address will be invalid. But minor defects in description, such as specifying one room too many, or a back garden that does not exist, are unlikely to lead to a decision that the notice is invalid; and if a notice to quit identifies the wrong address, it may be validated by a covering letter sent to the right one. The notice must be addressed to the tenant, although if only the first name is wrong this will not be enough to invalidate it. It may be enough to specify only one of two or more joint tenants (see 7 below) and it is certainly enough to serve it upon one only of the joint tenants. The notice must also state that it is given by or on behalf of the landlord, unless it is given by an agent acting in normal course of his business on the landlord's behalf when serving the notice.

In addition, a notice to quit from a landlord to a tenant who is a protected tenant (see Chapter 4) or a restricted tenant (see Chapter 5) must contain certain specified information, also in writing. Without this information the notice is invalid; a wholly invalid notice to quit a tenancy is, not to put too fine a point on it, not worth the paper it is written on. The information is as follows, although it does not have to be in the same form of words:

(i) Even after the notice to quit has run out the landlord

must get an order for possession from the court before the tenant can lawfully be evicted; and

(ii) If the tenancy is a protected tenancy under the Rent Act, the court can normally only give the landlord such an order on the grounds set out in the Act; and

(iii) Where the tenancy is not a protected tenancy, the tenant may be able to ask the rent tribunal to postpone the date when the notice to quit runs out for up to six months as long as he does so before the notice runs out; and

(iv) If the tenant does not know whether his tenancy is a protected tenancy or is otherwise unsure of his rights, he can obtain advice from a solicitor. Help with all or part of the cost of legal advice and assistance may be available under the Legal Aid Scheme. He can also seek information from a Citizen's Advice Bureau, a Housing Aid Centre, a rent officer or a Rent Tribunal Office.

Although at the end of a tenancy, a tenant becomes in strict, common law a trespasser, this is so untrue in practice as to be deceptive. A tenant who is a protected tenant (see Chapter 4) becomes a statutory tenant and, in effect, can remain on in the premises indefinitely, or subject only to proof of one of a limited number of sets of circumstances, until a court orders him to leave. This, and the right to registration of a fair rent for the tenancy, is considered in Chapter 4.

A restricted tenant is one who can refer his tenancy to the Rent Tribunal, both in respect of rent registration and also for deferrment of a notice to quit for up to six months at a time. This is considered in Chapter 5. *All* tenants are protected from eviction without due process of law, *i.e.* without a court decision which orders them to leave. Protected tenants are protected from eviction without court order by the Rent Act itself: all other tenants, even those who are not restricted tenants, are protected from eviction without a court order by the *Protection From Eviction Act 1977*. The position of tenants who are neither protected nor restricted, as regards both security and rent control, is considered in Chapter 6. Court proceedings must be *commenced* after the tenancy has expired, with one exception, dealt with in Chapter 5.

In order to establish, however, that there is a tenancy at all, then irrespective of the question of whether a tenancy was intended, it is necessary to establish that there are what is known as the four essential qualities of tenancy present. If one or more of them is missing, then the arrangement cannot be tenancy and for this reason will be that of licence. The four qualities are:

(i) *Identifiable parties*

There must be a landlord and a tenant. This does not mean that the tenant must know the identity of the landlord, for this is frequently unknown, where, for example, agents have granted the tenancy on behalf of the landlord. It means that a person cannot be a tenant either of himself, or of premises or land which have no owner. A person can, however, be a tenant of a company of which he is a director, or an employee, or even the major shareholder, and a person can be a tenant of a partnership of which he is one of the partners. In such a situation, it would be wrong to refer to the tenant alone as the owner: he is only the owner when taken together with the other partners. The same applies to trustees or joint owners. A person can also be a tenant of another who is himself no more than a tenant in the premises. Such a tenancy is called sub-tenancy and is dealt with below, 6.

(ii) *Identifiable Premises*

There must be premises of which to have a tenancy. This can be as little as a single room, or as much as several hundred acres of land. It is not, however, possible to be a tenant of part only of some premises, *e.g.* a shared room. It is possible to be a joint tenant with another of premises, (see 7 below); but if separate agreements have been reached with the landlord conferring on more than one person a right to occupy, *e.g.* a room, this cannot be tenancy because there is no identifiable part of the premises of which to have a tenancy. Even if the two, or more, individuals occupying were to divide up the room between themselves, they would still have to have access to the door in common. In this connection it is important, however, to bear in mind the caution concerning unsupportable evasive arrangements referred to in Chapter 1, and which will be referred to again (at 7, below).

(iii) *Period of Tenancy*

One cannot have a tenancy in respect of which there is no period of time involved. For that is exactly what tenancy is: a slice of time in the use of the premises. The one exception to this is a form of tenancy known as tenancy at will, but this is so rare that it can safely be ignored and, in this day and age, an arrangement which might once have attracted the title of tenancy at will is more likely to be considered a licence (*Heslop* v. *Burns*). The need to identify the period of the tenancy does not mean that a tenancy cannot in practice be granted for an indefinite time, for that is normally what happens when a periodic tenancy is granted. In these cases, the period for which the tenancy has been granted is the time of the periodic tenancy, *e.g.* one week, but the tenancy is automatically re-granted from week to week until determined by notice to quit.

(iv) *Exclusive Possession*

This is the most important, and often the hardest to establish of the four essential qualities of tenancy. It is hard to establish because even a licensee can have exclusive *occupation* of premises, and yet be considered no more than licensee. Exclusive *possession* means that the arrangement is intended to convey to the tenant the use to the exclusion of all others of the premises in question. This exclusive use is not destroyed because the landlord retains some right to visit, for example, to inspect for disrepair, or to collect the rent, nor, for example, because under the terms of the tenancy the landlord provides cleaning of the premises and a cleaner has access to the premises to carry out his duties. Such functions are visits to the premises, or services performed to or in the premises, but they are not *use* of them. The question is simply whether, in the terms or understanding of the arrangement, the premises are effectively being turned over for the period of the tenancy to the tenant. It may be that in the normal management of a hotel or a hostel, the landlord reserves the right to shift occupiers from room to room, as the occasion may demand. It is for this reason that the occupier cannot be described as having exclusive possession of the premises, even although he may have exclusive use of whatever room he is occupying for the time being. This is the "control" test: because the land-lord controls even the internal use of the premises, the tenant cannot be described as having exclusive possession.

Difficulties arise because it is at this quality of tenancy that landlords direct the most concerted attacks. The reservation of a right himself actually to use the premises, not merely to visit them, or to put in some other person to use them, would, if upheld by the court as a genuine term of the arrangement, effectively destroy the idea of exclusive possession. The over-riding principles described in Chapter 1 will be most relevant to this sort of arrangement. The court will apply them when deciding what was really intended, and just how much is an attempt to avoid protection by destroying the idea of tenancy itself. If a putative licence arrangement is held to constitute tenancy, then exclusive possession will automatically follow from that decision. Exclusive possession incorporates factual exclusive occupation, but exclusive occupation does not neces-sarily imply exclusive possession.

Possession if exclusive is exclusive as against the whole world, including the person who granted the tenancy, so that even a landlord commits a wrong by contravening his tenant's exclusive possession without permission. Such a wrong is a trespass and is dealt with in Chapter 8.

5. *Tied Accommodation*

A lot of people who live in accommodation which they do not own do so in accommodation which "goes with the job." Such people are not merely the obvious classes of service occupier or tenant, such as resident housekeepers, porters, au pairs, living-in help, caretakers, etc., but also such people as the managers of pubs and many who work in off-licences, employees of some of the nationalised industries, which together own consider-able housing stock, *e.g.* the railways, gas and electricity boards and the coal board, and even some teachers and social workers are provided with accommodation by local authorities, as an inducement to work in particular areas. The accommoda-tion is often job-related and the right to it customarily ends when the job itself is brought to an end.

Such classes of occupation pose particular problems in terms of housing law. Clearly, they do not constitute trespass or owner-occupation, and so must, of definition, be either tenancy or licence. But there are particular tests which apply in relation to tied accommodation. These tests exist *in addition* to those which we have already discussed: a person might appear to qualify as a tenant by application of one of the particular, job-related tests, and yet lack one of the four essential qualities of tenancy, or else be a licensee for some other reason, *e.g.* because on taking up new employment in a strange area, the employer offered to provide some temporary accommodation more-or-less as a favour. Unless, however, one of the prior tests applies, then the test which follows will determine whether occupation is by way of tenancy or licence. A service resident who is a licensee is called a "service occupier," and one who is a tenant is called a "service tenant."

In all these circumstances, it is assumed that the employment and the housing arrangements were reached as part of an overall package. It is entirely possible that a tenant subsequently becomes his landlord's employee. The tenancy would not then become service tenancy, anymore than it would if someone subsequently rented accommodation from his employer. It is also important to note that for these tests to come into operation, landlord and employer must be the same person in law. It is not uncommon for one person to, for example, own property in his own name, and to employ someone through a company, or a partnership. In law, a company or even a partnership constitutes a different "person" than its constituent "people." If a private landlord employs someone through a company, then the only reason that the accommodation will be treated as let on licence rather than tenancy will be either for one of the reasons mentioned above or because, despite the divergence in personality between landlord and employer, the court is prepared to accept that the arrangement in some way defeats the *intention* to grant a tenancy.

A person living in tied accommodation will be a service occupier if *either* it is necessary for him to live in the premises in question in order to carry out the employment duties, *or* it is a requirement of the contract of employment that he do so, and that requirement is imposed at the least for the better performance of employment duties, not merely as an arbitrary regulation, or whim, on the part of the employer. Indeed, it is not only possible but frequently happens that employers attach such conditions to a contract of employment in order to be able to let off property they happen to own without attracting Rent Act protection, *i.e.* they use their positions as employers as ways of entering into evasive arrangements. The normal overriding considerations will apply. If neither of the factors above applies, then, in the normal course of events, the occupier will be a service tenant.

Employees who occupy tied accommodation in agriculture and forestry occupy a peculiar position of privilege. Shortly, given certain qualifications, including length of employment in agriculture or forestry (but not necessarily with the same employer), despite the fact that they would normally qualify as service occupiers, they may come to enjoy full Rent Act protection as if they had tenancies. This, however, is outside the scope of this book. For further reading on this subject, see "Agricultural Tied Cottages," May 1977 L.A.G. Bulletin 111.

The problem that most commonly occurs in connection with occupiers of tied accommodation lies in establishing whether or not they are paying rent for their accommodation. Some will actually be doing so, *i.e.* they will be handing over a sum of money which will normally be entered as received in a rent book. This is likely to be the case where the nationalised industries are involved. Others may have an agreement as to how much rent they are putatively paying for their accommodation, but this may be deducted from their wages at source. Yet others may not have any agreed quantification of rent, but receive lower wages than they would normally get for the job in question on account of the provision of accommodation. Whether rent is actually being paid or not should not affect whether they are considered tenants or licensees, contrary to the normal presumption that one who pays no rent is not a tenant (*Heslop* v. *Burns.*)

6. *Subtenants*

As was remarked above, it is entirely possible that a person's landlord is himself no more than a tenant of another. In such a case, the "middle" tenant is known as a "mesne" (pronounced mean) tenant, and the "lower" tenant as the subtenant. Many more people are subtenants than realise it. In strict law, the owner who holds only on a long lease is a sort of tenant, although this classification is abandoned in considering classes of occupation, hence their inclusion as owner-occupiers. There are huge property holdings still in existence in which the interests are all held on leasehold. Indeed, it is not only possible but common for there to be many "intervening" interests by way of superior leasehold between an actual occupier and the ultimate freeholder.

So long as the mesne tenancy continues to exist, the subtenant is in no different position than any other tenant. His landlord must serve notice to quit in the normal way, and the subtenancy may fall into any of the classes of protection which will be discussed in Chapters 4 to 6. The position remains the same even when the mesne tenant is a protected tenant (see Chapter 4) and his contractual tenancy comes to an end. He becomes what is known as a statutory tenant, but the subtenant is unaffected by this.

Difficulties arise once the mesne tenant's interest comes to an end. This can be, in the case of a protected mesne tenant, when his contractual and statutory tenancies have come to an end, and in the case of an unprotected mesne tenant, *i.e.* one who is restricted (Chapter 5) or unrestricted (Chapter 6), once the contractual tenancy is determined in the normal way. In such a case, the question to be decided is whether the subtenant has any right to remain in occupation as against the superior landlord.

This will depend upon two main factors:

(i) Whether or not the mesne tenant and the subtenant are both protected tenants; and

(ii) Whether or not the subtenancy is a legal or illegal subtenancy.

The first point is one which can only be decided by reference to Chapter 4. However, it is fairly unlikely that a subtenant will be a protected subtenant because the principal condition which excludes a tenancy from protection is that the tenant lives in the same building as his landlord and most subtenants will indeed live in the same building as the mesne tenant who is, *vis-a-vis* the subtenant the landlord. If both mesne tenant and subtenant are protected by the Rent Act, however, *and* at the time the mesne tenancy comes to an end the subtenancy is legal, the subtenant will become the tenant of the landlord directly: Rent Act 1977 s. 137.

What is meant by an illegal subtenancy is that the terms of the mesne tenancy include a prohibition on subletting. Most written tenancies include such a term, and many weekly or monthly tenancies granted in the last few years and for which the terms are to be found in printed rent books provided by the landlord will also be subject to such a prohibition. Some prohibitions on subletting are absolute, *i.e.* they simply state that it is not permitted. Some are qualified, *i.e.* they state that it is not permitted without the consent of the landlord. The law implies into a qualified covenant a condition that such consent will not unreasonably be withheld and if a mesne tenant whose tenancy includes a qualified prohibition asks the landlord for consent and the landlord refuses without good reason, the law will override the refusal and consent will be deemed to be given. This can only happen if there has been a request and a refusal *before* the subletting is granted, which is extremely rare.

But even if an illegal subtenancy is created, it is possible that it will be subsequently "legalised." This can happen because the landlord learns of the illegal subletting and yet "waives" the breach of the terms of the tenancy by continuing to accept rent from the mesne tenant as if nothing had happened. It must be shown that the landlord knew there had been an actual subletting, for example, not, merely, that a friend had come to live with the mesne tenant, and waiver must be established, which is customarily taken to mean somewhat more than one accepted rent payment very shortly after the landlord found out. The knowledge of the landlord's employees, agents or officers is imputed to the landlord, so that if one such person knows of the illegal subletting and the landlord continues to accept rent there will have been a waiver. Waiver is considered further, in the discussion of Assignment, (9, below).

A mesne tenant who lets on an illegal subtenancy cannot himself subsequently take advantage of it. It is, after all, his wrong, or breach, not that of the subtenant. It is no ground for eviction of a subtenant by the mesne tenant that the letting was illegal. If there is nothing in the terms of the mesne tenancy which prohibits subletting, then by common law the mesne tenant is entitled to sublet. Once waiver has happened the subtenant becomes a legal subtenant as if in the first place he had been allowed in lawfully.

A subtenant who is not a protected subtenant, or one who is an illegal subtenant, whether or not protected, cannot take advantage of s. 137, in order to become the tenant of the landlord direct. However, if the mesne tenant himself surrenders to the landlord, and the landlord accepts the surrender (*Parker* v. *Jones*), or if the mesne tenancy comes to an end because the mesne tenant gives *valid* notice to quit to the landlord (*Mellor* v. *Watkins*), then the subtenant becomes tenant of the landlord regardless of whether or not the subtenancy is illegal, and regardless of whether protected. This is by operation of common law and operates also by way of waiver, although it takes place even when the landlord does not know of the existence of the subtenant. By accepting the surrender or notice to quit, the landlord is deemed to have waived any breaches by the tenant and to have taken over the tenant's liabilities, which include the subtenancy. This cannot happen if the mesne tenancy was already a statutory tenancy (see Chapter 4.)

A protected tenant who creates a lawful, protected subtenancy is obliged to notify the landlord of this in writing, within 14 days of creating the subtenancy, stating details of the subtenancy, including the name of the subtenant and the rent he is paying under the subtenancy (Rent Act 1977, s. 139.) Where the subtenant becomes tenant direct of the landlord by operation of s. 137, but not by operation of common law, then the landlord is entitled to disclaim responsibility for the provision of furniture, if he does so in writing within 6 weeks of the subtenant becoming his tenant (s. 138.)

All of these provisions, however, are dependent upon the subtenant being a tenant at all, and not merely a licensee. Someone who is the licensee of a tenant will find that his licence comes to an end automatically, without the giving of any notice, on the determination of the tenancy. Licensees of protected tenants (see Chapter 4) are then in the same position as someone who is a former licensee of the landlord direct, *i.e.* it may be that it is not necessary to take court proceedings to evict him. But the licensee of a tenant who is not protected is entitled to remain in occupation until a court order is sought against him: see Chapter 8. This anomaly was produced by legislative accident at the time the Rent Act 1974 was brought into force.

Whether or not a person is the licensee or subtenant of another will be a question of fact based on the normal considerations. But it is true to say that where the parties are living in the same premises, the court will look closely at the arrangement and unless there is clear evidence of separate living may well be inclined to view another occupier as a sharer, and as such a licensee, even although rent is paid, rather than a subtenant. Such clear evidence of separate living might be provided by a rent book, perhaps separate payment for gas and electricity, separate housekeeping, etc. This question, of whether a person is a licensee of someone he is sharing, for example, a flat with is considered further under the next heading.

7. *Joint Tenants*

A joint tenancy occurs wherever more than one person share the tenancy. Joint tenants do not each have a different part of, for example, a flat or a house: they are all equally entitled to share possession of the whole of it. Between them, they must establish the four essential qualities of tenancy, but they need not establish them (and, in particular, exclusive possession) as against each other. Joint tenants are each liable for the whole rent of the premises, so that if a landlord can only trace one of them, he will be obliged to pay any and all rent outstanding, even though he may subsequently be able to recover shares from any of the missing joint tenants. Married or cohabiting couples are frequently joint tenants, but so also are groups of friends. So long as they all remain together, acting, at least as against the landlord, in harmony, their position is exactly the same as that of a sole tenant. If there is any application, *e.g.* for rent registration, then they must either all sign the application, or else one of them must sign as agents for the others.

Service of a notice to quit on one is good service, although there is some doubt as to whether a notice to quit which identifies only one of the joint tenants as the tenant will be valid.

It is when the joint tenants themselves wish to go their separate ways that problems arise. If the tenancy is periodic, then one joint tenant can serve notice to quit and bring the contractual tenancy to an end, although if the tenancy is protected, this will not affect the right to security of tenure of the others: (see Chapter 4.) If it is fixed term, however, one alone cannot surrender it without the consent of the others. If one joint tenant simply departs, then the tenancy "devolves" on the remaining joint tenants.

Frequently, however, people who assume that they are joint tenants in fact, are not considered so in law. For example, a group of friends take a flat together, but only one of them is named in or signs the agreement, if any, or only one of them is named on the rent book. At first sight, the law would assume that the named occupier was the sole tenant, and that his sharers were either subtenants or licensees. It is possible to upset the first impression, with evidence that the entry of one name only was either oversight or intentionally inaccurate, by showing that the landlord was contracting with the whole group, and that it was clearly intended, as between themselves and as between them and the landlord, that they should all have equal rights in the premises. This might be witnessed by the fact that they each pay the rent for the whole of the premises to the landlord, in turn. But, consistently with the normal rule that it is intention which overrides all such questions, no single piece of evidence will be conclusive. It is hard to upset the first impression created by a written indication that the tenancy belongs to only one of them.

Will the occupiers then be licensees or subtenants? Again, the first impression that the law will receive is that a group of sharers are either joint tenants or, in the alternative, a sole tenant with a group of licensees. There is some merit to this attitude, for as between the group of occupiers it is infrequently indeed that they will have intended the formality of landlord and tenant. More likely, they are all sharing the outgoings, perhaps even buying food together, and living as one household. This would all suggest licence, rather than sub-tenancy. Subtenancy could be established, if there was clear evidence of separate living, as suggested above, under the last heading.

Another problem is posed by the use of the now common evasive device of "non-exclusive occupation agreements," referred to in Chapter 1. The technique of such an arrangement is that the landlord enters into a series of separate contracts with each occupier, granting to the occupier the right to use the premises in question in common with others, but no particular part of the premises. In this way, the landlord hopes to avoid a finding of tenancy of some part of the premises as against him, and because the agreements are all separate hopes also to avoid a finding of joint tenancy of the whole of the premises between himself and the group. Such evasive devices often purport to maintain for the landlord a right to come and live in the premises himself, or else to select new occupiers as and when one or other of the original group departs. The question is again one of intention: was it genuinely intended that this was the way the arrangement would work, or is it all merely a form of words designed to evade protection? In *Somma Hazelhurst and Ravelli* such an agreement was held to be effective to defeat protection as, on the facts of the particular case, the court considered that only separate licences had been granted.

If the group approach the landlord together, not as a series of separate individuals, and if the landlord looks to the group as a whole as responsible for the premises, then this is joint tenancy and the documents no more than shams. For example, if the landlord (as, indeed, will invariably be the case) expects the group to manage the interior of the premises, *e.g.* replacing light bulbs, even lavatory paper, paying bills for gas and electricity and perhaps telephone, perhaps looking after the interior decoration of the premises, then it is hard indeed to argue that as a group they do not have a tenancy, and exclusive possession against the landlord. To succeed in the use of such agreements, the landlord must establish that he is genuinely running the premises as some form of hostel, albeit that there is no resident manager, or that the separate agreements are wholly genuine as individual, and not inter-

dependent, contracts. A key factor will often be provided by
the landlord who, despite the fact that fewer than normal are
living in the premises, expects the group as a whole still to pay
the full amount of rent he customarily receives. The case of
Walsh and Walsh v. *Griffiths-Jones and Durant*, set out in full
in October 1977 LAG Bulletin 230 is an excellent study of this
sort of situation, of the attitude the courts are likely to take,
and of the relevant issues. The report was considered by the
Court of Appeal in *Somma* to be a "model analysis."

Once this series of hurdles is surmounted, and joint tenancy
established, the problems do not, unfortunately, end.
Commonly, in the course of time, one or more of the original
occupiers will drift on to alternative accommodation. What,
then, is the position of new occupiers, assuming that they are
selected by the occupiers themselves and not by the landlord?
If a new occupier is selected by the landlord, this will afford
the landlord excellent evidence that he is indeed in overall
possession of the premises and that therefore there can be no
tenancy at all.

If the landlord consents, a new occupier may become a joint
tenant with the others. If he does not, then the existing
occupiers cannot impose a new party to the tenancy on the
landlord against his will. The new occupier must be either subtenant or licensee and, given the remarks which have already
been made, is likely to be no more than licensee. In the course
of time, it may be that all the original occupiers will have left
and there will only be such licensees in occupation. The only
possible defence left is if the existing occupiers, or some of
them, can show that by the acceptance of rent the landlord has
accepted them as tenants, or as joint tenants.

8. *Tenants of Mortgagors*

A person is a tenant of a mortgagor when his landlord owns the
property, whether freehold or leasehold, under a mortgage. If
the landlord falls into arrears with mortgage repayments, the
mortgage company may "foreclose" and, in effect, take the
property over. It is in this situation that problems may arise for
the tenant. As long as the mortgagor remains in possession, the
tenant's position is wholly unaffected by the existence of a

mortgage on the property, even if the tenancy is granted in contravention of the terms of the mortgage.

For there are commonly prohibitions similar to those contained in tenancy agreements in the deeds of a mortgage. If a person owns property before taking a mortgage on it, which is not uncommon, then any tenancies existing at the date of the mortgage are unaffected by the deed. In such a case, even if the deed prohibits the creation of tenancies, on foreclosure the tenant will become the tenant of the mortgage company.

Almost all mortgage deeds prohibit the creation of tenancies, and the majority of tenancies of mortgagors are in fact created after the mortgage, so that there are very many tenants of mortgagors who are illegal tenants. This does not avail the mortgagor, of course, or afford him any additional right to evict the tenant. But if the mortgage company forecloses then no matter whether the tenant is protected or not, he has no right of occupation as against the mortgage company.

Even though the mortgage company knew of the illegal tenancy, but continued to accept repayments, there is no exact analogy with waiver of an illegal subtenancy. The only possibility is that after foreclosure the mortgage company either actively agrees to accept the continued presence of the tenant and takes on the tenancy, or it does so by implication by taking rent from the tenant over such a long period that the only inference that can properly be drawn is that it is treating the tenancy as binding upon itself.

9. *Assignees*

The term assignment has been used before, to describe the purchase of a long lease from the existing leaseholder. The same may occur in connection with lesser forms of tenancy, that is to say that one tenant may assign the tenancy to another. If there is nothing in the terms of the tenancy to prohibit this, then it is permissible. However, most tenancy agreements and rent books do include such prohibitions. Only a contractual tenancy can be assigned, *i.e.* not a statutory tenancy (see Chapter 4.) Strictly, like a surrender, it should be done by formal deed, but it can also operate either by way of what is known as part performance, or because the transaction is evidenced in writing, *i.e.* there is some written memorandum which provides an indication of what has taken place. Part performance means that the assignee, the person who has taken over the tenancy, has acted in such a way as could only be referable to an assignment, *e.g.* has spent considerable money on fixtures and fittings, or has redecorated the premises. An assignee steps into the shoes of the outgoing tenant, and occupies on exactly the same terms. There are prohibitions on what may be charged by one tenant to an incoming tenant, which are dealt with in Chapters 4 and 5.

An illegal assignee, that is to say one who has taken over in contravention of the terms of the tenancy agreement, may become legalised by waiver in the same way as an illegal subtenant can become a legal subtenant. An example of how this can happen is if the assignee starts paying rent to the landlord and, perhaps because of the size of the landlord's operation, which may even involve computerised rent processing, no one notices that someone new is paying the rent for some considerable time. Even a few rent payments, three or four perhaps, ought to be sufficient to establish waiver. In all cases of waiver, the crucial point to make is that a landlord cannot have his cake and eat it, by recouping rent for the premises, but retaining all the rights of eviction which an illegal transaction will afford him. The knowledge of the new tenant's presence need not be given in connection with rent payment, but could be, for example, because the assignee asks for repairs to be done and the landlord complies and, subsequently, goes on accepting rent. Again, the knowledge may be imputed to the landlord through information given to or acquired by his officers, employees or agents.

10. *New Landlords*

When a person purchases property, he does so subject to existing interests in it. A tenancy is an interest in property as, indeed, is a subtenancy, and even an illegal subtenancy. Accordingly, a purchaser takes subject to existing tenancies. A licence is not an interest in property, it is a personal right, and it would appear to be the case that a licence does not bind a new purchaser, although there is some contention about this

(*National Provincial Bank* v. *Ainsworth.*) The new landlord takes subject to all the old landlord's rights, liabilities and duties. He also takes liable to any knowledge the old landlord had, *e.g.* such knowledge as would found a claim for waiver of an illegal subtenancy or assignment. A tenancy dates from its original grant and there is no new tenancy on change of ownership. There are special provisions relating to change of ownership which apply to the question of whether or not a tenant has a resident landlord: Chapter 4. Before a tenant starts to pay rent to the new landlord, the old landlord should write to him, authorising the changeover.

Further Reading

"Tenant or Licensee," July 1974 LAG Bulletin 155.
"Subtenancies," March 1976 LAG Bulletin 62.
"Joint Tenants," May 1976 LAG Bulletin 132.
"Tenants of Mortgagors," June 1976 LAG Bulletin 132.
"A Note," August 1976 LAG Bulletin 183.
"A Note on Illegal Tenants of Mortgagors," February 1978 LAG Bulletin 33.

3 Owner-Occupation

In this chapter, we shall examine the rights of occupation of those who were described in Chapter 2 as owner-occupiers. As has already been remarked, the fullest status that anyone can enjoy is that of freehold owner-occupation, unencumbered by mortgage. He has to pay neither rent nor mortgage repayments and has an absolute right of occupation which can only be interfered with in the sorts of circumstances indicated in Chapter 2. The position of the freeholder and the leaseholder as regards mortgage repayments is substantially the same, and will be considered under the general heading of mortgages (below). In addition, the position of the leaseholder, whether or not the property is mortgaged, at the end of the lease must be considered.

The questions with which this Chapter are concerned, therefore, are:

1. *Leasehold Rights of Occupation*; and
2. *Mortgages.*

1. *Leasehold Rights of Occupation*

So long as a leasehold interest has not expired, an occupier has as full a right of occupation as a freeholder, and this can only be interfered with in the same ways referred to in Chapter 2. In fact so long as the occupier is using the premises, or part of them, as his home at the end of the lease, the lease will not automatically end and the occupier can remain in occupation indefinitely (*Landlord and Tenant Act, 1954, Part 1.*) The landlord can, however, serve a notice proposing that a statutory tenancy should come into existence. What this means is that he has brought the lease to an end, and that in its place there will be a statutory tenancy, exactly like that which a Rent Act protected tenant has at the end of his tenancy. This is described more fully in Chapter 4 but may be shortly described here, for these purposes, as the right to remain indefinitely in the premises unless and until the landlord can establish one of a specified series of grounds for possession, with which he can obtain a court order for possession. Those grounds are by and large the same as those for a Rent Act protected statutory tenant, but in addition the landlord can seek possession if he can prove that he proposes to demolish or reconstruct the whole or a substantial part of the premises in question. This is infrequently the case, especially since most such leasehold interests are in blocks of flats or terraced houses, in respect of which the leases may not end simultaneously. This restricts the capacity to redevelop.

There is, however, one additional form of protection which certain long leaseholders enjoy. Under the Leasehold Reform Act 1967, a person who is a long leaseholder of a house, but not of a flat, can compel the landlord to sell him the freehold of the premises, or else can compel the landlord to extend the lease for a further 50 years beyond the date of its original termination. These rights only apply to those houses which are not horizontally divided from any other premises, *i.e.* they do not, to any extent, overlap or, as it were, underlap another property. The house need not, however, be freestanding: it could be in a row of terraced houses.

A leaseholder must exercise these rights *before* the lease expires and the landlord serves a notice proposing a statutory tenancy but can only do so if, at the time the right to purchase the freehold (known as enfranchisement) or to extend the lease (extension) is claimed, the leaseholder has been occupying the house as his only or main residence for a period of at least five years. It is enough to occupy only part of the premises, *e.g.* if the occupier has the lease on a whole house, lives in part and lets out part this will suffice. The purpose of the residential qualification is to prevent speculation.

The price of the purchase can be fixed, failing agreement between the parties, by the Lands Tribunal, but the procedure is very complicated and anyone intending to use it should consult a lawyer or surveyor. Unlike proceedings before most other tribunals, legal aid is available to pay for the cost of a lawyer and a surveyor or valuer before the Land Tribunal: see, generally, Appendix 2. Extension does not cost anything, although a new ground rent (*i.e.* low rent) which is appropriate to the value of the house at the date when the new lease starts will be fixed to take effect from that date. Extension is provided mainly for those who cannot afford to enfranchise or who, perhaps being elderly and with no relatives to whom to leave any acquired interest, have no reason to do so.

Enfranchisement can be extremely cheap. All that is being bought back is the benefit of a very small ground rent (usually in single figures for a whole year) and the fairly remote possibility that the landlord will ever get the property back at all. The longer there is to run on the lease at the time a notice indicating an intention to purchase is served, the cheaper the price will be because the landlord's expectations are the more remote. It follows that as soon as an occupier has fulfilled the residential qualification, he should exercise the power to enfranchise as soon as possible. The price of enfranchisement bears no relation at all to current property values or even to the customarily lower than vacant possession value at which many sitting tenants are permitted to buy from their landlords. It may be a figure of less than £100, or not much more.

In this connection, perhaps more than in any other, legal advice should be treated with some caution. Few lawyers are familiar with the mechanics of enfranchisement, or the very low prices at which the properties can be bought. Many people accept the advice of a lawyer that a landlord's initial asking price should be accepted without bothering to go through the formal procedures. Lawyers may give this advice because, in comparison to the property values in which they are more accustomed to deal, they think that a figure of, *e.g.* £500, is as low as possible. The advice of a surveyor will count for much more than that of a lawyer as regards enfranchisement.

2. *Mortgages*

Both freehold and leasehold owner-occupation can, and frequently will, be subject to a mortgage. Although all mortgage deeds contain a variety of terms (*e.g.* not to create tenancies in the property without permission, see Chapter 2), it is usually only when an occupier falls into arrears with the repayments that the company has a right to foreclose on the mortgage.

Before legal proceedings are started, the mortgage company will normally make a written demand for any arrears of repayment. It is not obliged by law to do this, but in practice the court (which has discretionary powers which are described below) will not look kindly upon a mortgage company which has leapt to exercise its full legal rights without warning the occupier and giving him a chance to redeem the position. If the arrears are paid off at that point, nothing further will normally happen. If an occupier has a bad history of arrears, however, the mortgage company may still decide to press on with the full legal procedure.

After any demand for the arrears, there will be a formal demand for repayment of the whole of the outstanding debt. This will be for all capital outstanding, and also any accumulated interest. At this point, an occupier can, if he is in a position to do so, buy off the mortgage company entirely, and retain possession of the property. There has to be such a formal demand, even if it is quite obvious that the occupier cannot comply with it.

The next step is for the mortgage company to issue possession proceedings in the county court: see Appendix 1. They cannot evict the occupier without court proceedings. The court is not obliged to grant the possession order immediately. It has power to grant an order suspended on condition that the occupier continues to pay current instalments under the mortgage, and a fixed amount per payment off the arrears. Suspended orders are considered in Appendix 1.

The court will only exercise this discretion if it is of the view that the arrears can be cleared in a reasonable time. If it does not think this can be done, then the order will be final, but will usually be suspended for at least 28 days to give the occupier time to start making alternative arrangements: see Chapter 10, Homelessness.

There is no formal definition of reasonable time. The courts normally consider one year a reasonable time in which to clear the arrears. So far as a private mortgage company is concerned, if the arrears cannot be cleared in a year, or not much more, there is not a lot that can be done, unless the company itself is amenable to repayment over a longer period. The courts tend to regard mortgage companies as bound only by the normal rules of business ethics and private enterprise, and are therefore reluctant to impose upon them the effects of individual hardship.

This is not necessarily the case where public authorities are concerned. Many mortgages are granted by local authorities. Local authorities are not well-known for the speed with which they operate. It is common for the first letter demanding arrears to arrive at a time when an occupier owes only a two-figure amount. But it may be a year or even more before the next letter arrives. This may be a further demand for the arrears, or it may be the final and formal demand for full repayment of the outstanding debt. In either event, the arrears will by then probably be a three-figure amount, and beyond what an occupier can hope to pay off within a year, at the same time as having to maintain current instalments. While the courts will not regard this behaviour on the part of the local authority as blameworthy, many will accept that public authorities have a slight duty to chase occupiers. They may be prepared to accept that such "contributory dilatoriness" should not result in an outright order for possession and, therefore, that repayment of the arrears can take place over a longer period of time, even as much as two or three years.

Normally, a social worker will not attempt or purport to represent a client in court. A social worker has, of course, no right of audience in a court, *i.e.* no right to represent someone; but the court has power to hear anyone at the request of one of the parties. It will not take kindly to intervention by a social worker on a point of law, and if a social worker has anything to say about the facts of a case, then he will do so as a witness. But where what is concerned is the exercise of a discretion by the court, then it is unlikely to resent the representations or explanations of an occupier's social worker. A social worker may, therefore, be able to persuade a court to use its discretion towards an occupier more generously than it might at first be inclined to do, for example, by impressing upon the court the extent of hardship to a particular occupier, or, perhaps, by being able to explain why what at first appears to be irresponsible or blameworthy behaviour by an occupier is in fact the result of circumstances beyond his control.

Many occupiers will have financial difficulties far too serious to be solved by a suspended order for possession and periodic repayment of arrears over a year or two. Indeed, such an obligation can often lead them further into financial difficulty. It may be that more drastic measures are desirable. Steps can be taken to avert arrears at an early stage and so avoid court proceedings altogether, if action is taken as soon as it appears that an occupier is running into financial difficulty.

For example, rearrangement of a mortgage can increase the amount which an occupier who is in receipt of Supplementary Benefit (Chapter 7) will receive by way of regular allowance. Similarly, it may be possible to approach a mortgage company with a proposal for rearrangement or for a temporary arrangement in order to bide an occupier over a period of particularly acute financial hardship. With these possibilities in mind, an outline knowledge of how mortgages work will be of some help:

All mortgages are a form of loan against the security of the property in question. In all cases, the mortgage company wants back the capital sum loaned, and interest on it for the period for which it has been lent. Mortgages can be arranged for repayment over any period of time, although they are usually arranged for repayment over a period from 15 to 25 years.

There are two principal sorts of mortgage:

(i) *Capital repayment mortgage*

A capital repayment mortgage is a loan which requires repayment in periodic amounts which are assessed in at least two and commonly three parts. Although it is not an essential part of a capital repayment mortgage, most reputable mortgage companies insist that there is included in the package an element of insurance, called the mortgage protection policy. This provides insurance against the death of the owner-occupier, in which case the insurance will pay off any outstanding mortgage and so leave the property unencumbered for the next-of-kin.

The two essential parts of the repayments are capital repayment and interest. Monthly payments are assessed at an amount slightly larger than the interest due on the original capital loan. This means that at the beginning of a mortgage repayment period, an owner-occupier is not paying back much of the capital but is mostly paying interest on it. Gradually, however, the capital will decrease. The monthly payments remain the same, except for fluctuations in the rate of mortgage interest. In later years, therefore, when the amount of capital outstanding has been reduced, the monthly payment covers a smaller sum due by way of interest, and a correspondingly larger amount of capital repayment. In the final years of a mortgage, there is little interest due at all, and most of the payment is capital repayment.

(ii) *Endowment mortgage*

The monthly payment under an endowment mortgage is a sum assessed in two parts only — interest repayment, and life assurance premium. Subject to fluctuations in the mortgage interest rate, both these amounts remain the same. There is no capital repayment. Instead, the life assurance premium guarantees that either at the end of the period for which the mortgage has been taken out, or on the death of the mortgagor, the insurance company will pay off the whole of the capital outstanding. There are other benefits which may be included in an endowment mortgage deal.

It is generally well-known that there will be tax relief on mortgage interest. This, at least, is so provided that the purpose of the mortgage was home purchase or home improvement. It will not be available if the mortgage was taken out because of some other financial need. Tax relief is available to the full amount of the interest payments. It is allowed in addition to an individual's other personal tax allowances. In effect, it reduces the cost of the interest to the mortgagor by the amount of whatever is the current rate of income tax, in 1977-78, 34 per cent.

There is a less well-known alternative to tax relief. This is called the government option scheme. People will normally select either tax relief or the government option scheme at the time that they take out the mortgage. A person who selects government option does not receive any tax relief on interest payments under the mortgage. Instead, the mortgagor is charged only a proportion of the interest he would normally pay, and the government pays the balance directly to the mortgage company. This is available whether the mortgage is capital payment or endowment.

There are several possible rearrangements of mortgage affairs which may be appropriate in different situations:

(a) Tax relief is of no use at all to someone who does not pay tax, *e.g.* because his earnings are too low, or because he has no earnings at all. If an owner-occupier has selected tax relief and subsequently his income falls to the point where there is no benefit because no or not enough tax is being paid, then it will be financially advantageous to switch to government option. This can be done at any time, although a person already on government option cannot switch to tax relief until four years after the start of the mortgage.

(b) Capital repayment mortgages are usually slightly cheaper than endowment mortgages. At a time of financial hardship, therefore, it may be advisable to switch from one to the other.

(c) Another rearrangement of affairs which may reduce immediate costs applies only to capital repayment mortgages. In the later years, the interest element of a monthly repayment is fairly low. It may be possible to persuade a mortgage company to, as it were, regrant the mortgage so that the capital outstanding is payable over a longer number of years than originally intended. This will not affect the interest payments, for the amount of capital outstanding is the same, but it will spread the capital repayments over that many more years. It follows that the capital portion of monthly repayments will be reduced and this will lead to an overall reduction, which may not, however, be very large, in the monthly payments.

(d) It may be that a period of financial hardship is, even at the outset, of an identifiably limited period. For example, when a relationship breaks up (see Chapter 9), there will often be a period during which a wife is not receiving any adequate maintenance from her husband, while at the same time she remains liable for all the normal household outgoings. A mortgage company is bound to accept repayments from a wife, even although the property is in the name of the husband. A court may order the transfer of the property from one name

into another. These questions are dealt with in Chapter 9, but
while they are being sorted out, a wife may be able to persuade
the mortgage company to accept payments of interest only,
and nothing at all off the capital, to give her, as it were, some
sort of breathing space.

(e) Some occupiers have not one, but two mortgages on their
properties. This might have happened, for example, because
an occupier needed money to improve an already mortgaged
property and approached some other company to advance him
the funds. The correct procedure would be to approach a local
authority for a maturity loan, which is an interest only loan
subject to a charge on the property, which the authority
realises either on death of the borrower or on sale of the house.
Maturity loan is described in greater detail in the book
Housing: Repairs and Improvements. But an occupier may
not have been aware of this possibility or, for some other
reason, may have been refused a loan by the authority. Second
mortgages command higher rates of interest than do first
mortgages because, if the property has to be sold to get the
loan back, the first mortgage company will take priority out of
the proceeds of sale. It is possible that at a time of financial
hardship, the first mortgage company may, as it were, take
over the second mortgage and consolidate the whole of the
loan into one, at the lower rate of interest.

Most of these rearrangements cannot be imposed on a mortgage company against its will. Nonetheless, there is nothing to
stop an occupier approaching the company with a request;
and the clearer the proposals that he can make, the greater are
the chances of success. The larger, more reputable mortgage
companies do not, as a matter of course, want to see occupiers
evicted and the properties sold. Their money comes, after all,
from keeping mortgages in existence and receiving interest on
them. Less reputable mortgage companies, many of whom
charge interest rates as high as 28 per cent., are less responsible
and less amenable to rearrangement.

Further Reading

Tunnard J. and Whately C., (CPAG/SHAC) *Rights Guide for Home Owners*.

4 Full Security

In this Chapter, we shall examine the Rent Act protected tenancy, the rights of the protected tenant to security of tenure and to regulation of rent paid, and some further financial protection. It is only *tenants* who can enjoy full, Rent Act protection, not trespassers or licensees nor, except as described in Chapter 3, owner-occupiers. In the main, tenants whose landlords are not public bodies, such as the Crown or a local authority, nor quasi-public bodies, such as Housing Trusts and Registered Housing Associations, will be protected tenants provided that their landlords do not live in the same building as themselves. This short description can, however, be misleading as some who would appear to qualify will not be protected tenants, and others who would appear to be excluded may, for one reason or another, in fact enjoy full protection.

Protected tenants may be regulated tenants, or they may be controlled tenants, depending principally on the date when the tenancy began. Controlled tenancies are easily identified by the very low rents paid. In addition, all protected tenants may be contractual tenants, or they may be statutory tenants. Security of tenure provides, in effect, a right or status of irremovability after the normal determination of a tenancy. Before determination of the tenancy, the tenant is known as a contractual tenant; after, during the continuation of the right of occupation, he is known as a statutory tenant. A statutory tenancy continues on exactly the same terms as the prior contractual tenancy, save where such terms would be inconsistent with the idea of statutory tenancy, for example a right to assign or sublet the whole of the premises, and save as regards rent which, obviously, may be increased as the years pass.

Normally, a tenant will be first a contractual tenant and subsequently a statutory tenant. This may not be the case, however, when a protected tenant dies and a member of his family, or his widow, succeeds to the tenancy. In such circumstances, the successor becomes a statutory tenant at once, and the terms are the same, save as already mentioned, as those of the contractual tenancy of the person to whom the new tenant has succeeded.

Under the present legislation, the Rent Act 1977, such succession can take place twice after the death of the original tenant. If the tenant who dies is a man who leaves a widow, she will have priority in the succession. If this is not the case, then any member of the family who was residing with the tenant at the time of the tenant's death and for six months beforehand is entitled to succeed to the tenancy. If the original tenant was a woman who left a husband, then it is under this second limb that the widower will succeed to the tenancy. Family is construed broadly, so that even a cohabitee of some long-standing can succeed to the tenancy: *Dyson Holdings Ltd* v. *Fox*. The test is whether people generally would have regarded the couple as "family," even although they were not married in law. Friends with a platonic relationship, cannot be termed family, no matter how long they have lived together: *Joram Developments Ltd.* v. *Sharratt*. When the second successor himself dies, the landlord is entitled to reclaim possession of the premises, although, of course, he may be willing to grant a new course, he may be willing to grant a new tenancy in any event.

The distinction between a contractual tenancy and a statutory tenancy may not be without importance, as regards both security of tenure and rent regulation. This is especially so if the contractual tenancy is a fixed-term tenancy. Before any court proceedings to evict the tenant can be brought, on one or other of the grounds described below, the contractual tenancy must have been brought to an end. Even if a tenant is in arrears of rent, then it will be necessary for the landlord to forfeit a fixed-term agreement, or serve valid notice to quit. Unless he does so, then no matter how great the tenant's default, the proceedings will be wholly defective and no order will be made. The tenancy must have expired by the date proceedings are commenced, not just by the date of hearing.

The tenant may be able to derive similar advantage as regards rent from a lengthy fixed-term tenancy. Although normally the registration of a fair rent will result in a decrease in the amount the landlord is entitled to charge, on occasion it will actually increase beyond that which the landlord and the tenant have agreed between them. In such circumstances, the landlord will still be limited by the contractual rent, until such time as he can bring the contractual tenancy to an end. The mere fact that there has been such an increase will not affect, for example, an agreement that the tenant shall occupy for three years at a particular, and lower, rent. For this reason, many fixed-term agreements now say that the contractual rent will be a particular sum *or* the registered rent, if that is higher. Such a clause is wholly valid.

To bring the contractual tenancy to an end, a landlord must determine the tenancy in the normal way, *e.g.* forfeiture, expiry of fixed term or valid notice to quit containing the prescribed information, all of which procedures have been described in Chapter 2. Thereinafter, there is no need to serve any further notice before bringing proceedings, even if there is a gap of several years between termination of the contractual tenancy and the commencement of proceedings. No new contractual tenancy comes into being, unless there is evidence that this was intended, *e.g.* because the landlord and the tenant agreed to vary some term of the tenancy other than rent and it is sufficiently substantial to warrant description as a new tenancy. Normally, the tenant simply occupies as a statutory tenant until such time as a court may order possession to be given up to the landlord.

The distinction between regulated and controlled tenancies, both of which can and at some time probably will be either contractual or statutory tenancies, is one which relates only to rent and does not affect security of tenure at all. Briefly, controlled tenants are subject to a form of rent regulation known as "rent control," which sets the limit of rent chargeable at a figure related to the rateable value of the property at a certain, specified date. Regulated tenancies, which the majority of protected tenancies will now be, are subject to the "fair rent" system, which is a rent limit fixed by an official known as the Rent Officer. Fair rents are much higher than controlled rents.

All protected tenancies will be regulated rather than controlled tenancies *unless*:

(i) The rateable value of the premises on November 7, 1956 did not exceed £40 (City of London or Metropolitan Police

District) or £30 (elsewhere); *and*

(ii) The premises were not built or produced by conversion completed after August 29, 1954; *and*

(iii) The original contractual tenancy was not a tenancy for more than 21 years; *and*

(iv) The original tenancy started before July 6, 1957.

However, a number of controlled tenancies have been *converted* into regulated tenancies. This can have happened in one of a number of ways:

(i) If the rateable value of the premises on March 31, 1972 was £95 or more (Greater London) or £60 or more (elsewhere), automatic conversion took place on January 1, 1973; *or*

(ii) If the rateable value of the premises on March 31, 1972 was £80 or more (Greater London) or £45 or more (elsewhere), automatic conversion took place on July 1, 1973; *or*

(iii) If the rateable value of the premises on March 31, 1972 was £70 or more (Greater London) or £35 or more (elsewhere), automatic conversion took place on January 1, 1974; *or*

(iv) If there have been two successions to the original tenancy, the tenancy became regulated on the second succession; *or*

(v) The landlord has applied for and the local authority has granted a "qualification certificate" to the effect that the premises are equipped with all the standard amenities, are in good repair and are in all other respects fit for human habitation.

The standard amenities are a sink, a fixed bath or shower, a wash-hand basin, a hot and cold water supply to all of these, and a WC, for the exclusive use of the tenant. All of these should normally be inside the dwelling. A tenant whose landlord is seeking such a certificate will be served with a notice and will have an opportunity to object if the premises do not satisfy these conditions. A tenant is entitled to refuse to permit his landlord to carry out works in order to satisfy the conditions before applying for the certificate. A tenant may do this because he is happy with what he is familiar with, or else because he does not want to pay the higher rent that will certainly follow conversion to regulation.

In such a case, all that the landlord can do is obtain from the local authority a provisional certificate which will specify the works which have to be carried out before the certificate becomes fully effective, and the landlord will then have to seek an order from the county court permitting him to enter and do the works. The tenant may appear at court and object to this and the court will consider his position, especially with regard to health and age. Alternative accommodation will have to be made available for the tenant while works are carried out.

If the local authority refuses to issue a full qualification certificate, because it does not believe that the qualifications have been met, the landlord will have a right of appeal to the county court where, again, the tenant has a right to be heard.

It is possible that a few tenancies which fall within the first three classes of tenancy subject to automatic conversion, on January 1, 1973, July 1, 1973, and January 1, 1974, may *not* have been converted if, at least three months before decontrol was due, *either*

(i) The local authority had served a notice under section 16 Housing Act 1957 to the effect that the premises had been found to be unfit for human habitation; *or*

(ii) The local authority had made a compulsory purchase order following inclusion of the premises in a clearance area; *or*

(iii) The local authority had made a clearance order; *or*

(iv) The premises has been declared unfit under the Land Compensation Act 1961.

If, however, before March 11, 1975, the dwelling had been declared fit again, or excluded from a clearance area, or the clearance order did not proceed, then the automatic conversion took place whenever this happened. But if none of these things had happened by March 11, 1975, the conversion would not have taken place at all and the tenancy would still be controlled unless it had been converted for one of the other reasons described above *i.e.* second succession or qualification.

There are only about 2,000 controlled tenancies left in the country and their occupants are mostly elderly people, many of whom are living alone and in straitened circumstances. The Department of the Environment suggests (Rent Act Consultation Paper) that many if not most of the landlords under such tenancies will themselves also be far from well-off and may be individuals who have inherited one or two properties from their parents. Such landlords are the ones who have the greatest difficulty keeping property in repair and will also be those receiving the lowest rents. In such circumstances, you should have regard to the possibilities of grant-aided improvement and purchase consequential upon service of a compulsory improvement notice, described in the book *Housing: Repairs and Improvements.*

Particular problems of definition may apply to those who occupy premises part of which consist of, for example a shop or business. If the tenancy otherwise qualifies as a controlled tenancy, then it will be protected; but if it does not, then it will be given some degree of protection by alternative legislation, the Landlord and Tenant Act 1954, Part 2, which is principally concerned with business tenancies and, as such, outside the scope of this book. For further reading on this subject, see "Tenancies With Mixed Business and Residential Use," March 1977 LAG Bulletin 58.

The rest of this Chapter will be taken up with the following questions:

1. *Who is a protected tenant?*
2. *What security of tenure do protected tenants have?*
3. *What rent protection applies?*
4. *Other forms of financial protection.*

1. *The Protected Tenant*

The Rent Act assumes that *all tenants* are protected tenants *unless* there is some factor which takes them out of protection. Some of those excluded from protection will be subject to the jurisdiction of the Rent Tribunal and, as such, will be dealt with in Chapter 5. Others will be subject to no statutory protection and will be able to rely only upon provisions of the common or case-law. These are dealt with in Chapter 6. The factors which take a tenancy out of protection deal with:

(i) In respect of tenancies commencing on or after August 14, 1974, whether the landlord lives in the same building or not (Rent Act 1977, s.12);

(ii) In respect of tenancies commencing before August 14, 1974, whether the tenancy was considered to be a furnished tenancy in law before that date, and whether the landlord has lived in the same building or not since August 14, 1974 (Sched. 24);

(iii) Regardless of when the tenancy commenced, whether the tenant shares living accommodation with the landlord or not (section 21);

(iv) Whether the tenant is provided with attendances (section 7);

(v) Whether the tenant is provided with board (section 7);

(vi) Whether the rent is what the law knows as a "low rent" (section 5);

(vii) Whether it is a student letting (section 8);

(viii) Whether any rent is paid (section 5);

(ix) Whether it is a holiday letting (section 9);

(x) The identity of the landlord (sections 3-16);

(xi) The rateable value of the premises (section 4).

(i) *Tenancies commencong on or after August 14, 1974*

When the Rent Act 1974 came into operation, on 14 August 1974, it brought with it two major changes. One has already been referred to (Chapter 1), which is to say that it extended full Rent Act protection to the tenants of furnished accommodation. The other was that it created a new class of tenancy subject to the lesser security of the Rent Tribunal: these are tenants whose landlords occupy another part of the same building (not being a purpose-built block of flats) as their residences.

For a landlord to take advantage of this exemption to protection, he must establish that at all times since the commencement of the tenancy, he has used the other part of the building which he occupies as a residence. The law accepts that a person may have more than one residence at a time, but a purely token residence will not suffice: a landlord cannot simply keep one room in a house, or in several houses, in order to keep his tenants out of protection. The question that must be asked is not whether at all times the landlord has been *in* residence, or has resided in the part kept for himself, but whether the premises have been *a* legal residence of the land-lord throughout the period in question, *i.e.* since the start of the tenancy. Legal residence is discussed in greater detail under 2, below, for the same test applies to the question of whether a statutory tenant has sustained sufficient residence to maintain his right to the statutory tenancy. Briefly, residence means that premises are being used as a home, even if not the only home. However, it is accepted that for short periods a person may cease to use premises as a residence and still be treated as sustaining legal residence, provided *both* that he fully intends to return to live in the premises, *and* that he has left some physical signs of occupation in the premises, *e.g.* furniture, belongings, family.

A corporate landlord, *i.e.* a landlord which is a company, a trust, a partnership, etc., cannot "reside" at all because such a landlord has no natural life.. It is thought that residence by one of two or more joint owners/landlords is enough to keep the tenant out of protection. Purpose-built blocks of flats means exactly what it says: a house converted into flats, no matter how long ago, or however separately the living units are now constructed, even if there are separate entrances, will not be a purpose-built block. If the building is a purpose-built block, however, then it avails the landlord not at all that he lives in one and the tenant lives in another flat.

If a landlord sells the house, residence will nonetheless be treated as continuing for a further 14 days. If, during that time, the new owner serves notice that he intends to move into the premises for use as a home, then he has a total of six months in which to do so, during which period also, residence by the landlord will be treated as continuing. If by the end of the six months the new owner has not taken up residence, the tenant will become a protected tenant and will so remain, even when the owner moves in, for there will not have been continual residence since the start of the tenancy.

The position is somewhat different on the death of a resident landlord. In such circumstances, the executors effectively have one year in which to sell to a new resident landlord who must move in within that time. If this happens, residence will have been treated as continuing throughout the period but, during the period when there is in fact no resident landlord in occupation, the tenant is treated *as if* protected and can only be evicted if one of the grounds appropriate to the eviction of a protected tenant is established; see 2., below. If no landlord moves in within the period, the tenant becomes and remains protected.

The reason for this difference is quite easily explained: the tenants of resident landlords are normally entitled to apply to the Rent Tribunal for security of tenure, for up to six months at a time: (see Chapter 5). If, therefore, a new owner purchases a house and serves notice of intention to move in but at the same time serves notice to quit, it should be possible for the tenant to gain enough security from the Rent Tribunal to stay until the end of the six months. It will then be known whether in fact the new owner is going to take up residence, or is really trying to gain vacant possession for the purpose of resale. However, six months would not be an adequate period to dispose of a property on the death of a resident landlord, in view of the complications of executorship.

Note

In certain circumstances, a tenant who would appear to have been excluded from protection because of (i), above, may in fact be protected for technical reasons:

(a) Former Protected Tenants

A landlord with a good knowledge of the law might be able to take protection away from a tenant, *e.g.* by moving into a house in which there is an existing protected tenant and offering him a new tenancy of the same or another part of the building, so as to claim that since the start of *that* tenancy, there has always been a resident landlord. The Rent Act s. 12 provides that a tenant who was *formerly* a protected tenant under a previous tenancy of the *same* or *another* part of the building remains a protected tenant. This, however, is only so where the presence of the resident landlord is the only reason for exclusion from protection.

(b) Fixed Term Second Tenants

This is another odd rule, and one that has been designed to deal with a rather particular situation. A tenant who is excluded from protection by reason only of the presence of a resident landlord will be a restricted tenant (see Chapter 6.) Restricted tenants who have periodic tenancies can refer any notice to quit to a body known as the Rent Tribunal which can defer the notice for up to six months at a time. Fixed term restricted tenants cannot do this. The law considers it fair that a landlord taking a tenant into his own home should be able to set a period, during which he will decide whether or not he wants the tenant to go on living in the premises. This can be a fixed term tenancy. Alternatively, a landlord can grant a periodic tenancy and take the comparatively minor risk that the Rent Tribunal will defer a notice to quit for up to six months. What the law does not permit the landlord to do is to have his cake and eat it by retaining a good tenant, but depriving him of any prospect of Rent Tribunal security by keeping him on a string of short fixed term tenancies. Alternatively, the law will not permit a landlord to evade the prospect of a six month extension of a notice by persuading the tenant to accept, for example a three month fixed term tenancy. Accordingly, any tenant excluded from protection by reason only of the presence of a resident landlord, and who has a fixed term tenancy, will be and remain a protected tenancy if he was the tenant, whether periodic or fixed term, of the same or another part of the building. The earlier tenancy must itself have been excluded from protection only by reason of the presence of a resident landlord.

(ii) *Tenancies commencing before August 14, 1974*

As was remarked in Chapter 1, the general policy of the legislature is to not remove protection from anyone who already has it. It follows that questions may still arise, in connection with tenancies commencing before the Rent Act 1974 came into force, as to whether or not the tenant was protected before that date. If he was *not*, then the question arises as to whether there has been a resident landlord since that date. The test for this is exactly as described under the last heading.

Deciding whether or not premises were protected prior to August 14, 1974 is no easy business. The class exempted from protection was that of furnished tenancies. But the law did not consider that any amount of furniture would take a tenant out of protection. The landlord had to provide so much furniture that the value *to the tenant* of the furniture forms a substantial proportion of the whole rent paid under the tenancy. For some years, it was considered that, notwithstanding the intricacy of this formula, a tenant would nonetheless be treated as a furnished tenant if a substantial amount of furniture was provided. It is, of course, perfectly possible to provide a substantial amount of furniture without any great expenditure or, indeed, without providing anything of much value to the tenant. In the case of *Woodward* v. *Docherty*, however, decided only a matter of months before the 1974 Act came into force, the Court of Appeal accepted two important propositions: first of all, that it was correct to do a financial calculation of the value to the tenant of the furniture, so that even a substantial amount of furniture could leave the tenant protected; and secondly, that in calculating the value of the furniture *to the tenant*, regard may be had to the social conditions prevailing at the time. This meant that rather than acquiring some valuable and desirable asset by way of use of furniture, the tenant in fact lost the considerably more valuable asset of a protected tenancy, while the landlord gained by being able to evict his tenant with little or no difficulty. In other words, the Court of Appeal recognised that the purpose of the provision of furniture was not to benefit the tenant, but rather to benefit the landlord.

As this question can still commonly occur, especially amongst those a social worker is likely to encounter in his work, it is worthwhile being familiar with the correct approach to a furniture valuation. The first stage is to calculate the value to the tenant of the furniture, not the cost to the landlord. A second-hand dealer is the best person to help you do this and, as a rough-and-ready guide, what he values the furniture at will represent the value to the tenant; it is that amount which the tenant would have to pay to provide similar furniture of his own.

The valuation is done as if it was being established as at the start of the tenancy. Having established this basic figure, take a percentage, which is customarily agreed at 20 per cent., which represents the fair return to the landlord on his notional investment in that valuation. It is this figure which is to be compared to the annual rent paid by the tenant at the outset of the tenancy and which must be considered from the point of view of substantiality. There is no legislative guideline as to what does form a substantial proportion of the rent, but courts will normally view anything over 20 per cent. as substantial, anything between 15 per cent. and 20 per cent. as probably substantial, anything between 15 per cent. and 10 per cent. as possibly substantial, and anything below 10 per cent. as insubstantial. In the grey areas, such questions as how much furniture is provided may influence the court.

On the basis of this calculation, it will be possible to decide whether the tenancy was protected or not at the start of the tenancy, *i.e.* whether or not it was furnished in law. If it was protected, then the tenant remains a protected tenant, even though there has been a resident landlord in the building since August 14, 1974; if it was not, then the question will be whether he has been protected since that date. Neither the test contained under this heading, nor that contained under the last, will be applicable if the conditions specified under (iii) below take the tenant out of protection.

The "second tenancy" provisions described in the *Note* to (i) above, do not apply if the tenancy is excluded from protection for this reason, *i.e.* was granted before August 14, 1974, was furnished in law, and since that date there has been a resident landlord: *Stubbs* v. *Assopardi and Another*. Neither of the provisions will apply if the reason for the exclusion from protection is one of those which follow.

(iii) *Sharing living accommodation with landlord*

If the tenant shares what the law recognises as living accommodation with his landlord, then regardless of when the tenancy commenced, it will not be a protected tenancy. This is so even if no furniture at all was provided under the tenancy, and also even if the degree of residence by the landlord leaves in some doubt whether he qualifies as a resident landlord in the normal way. However, a mere empty retention of a right to share living accommodation, designed to defeat protection, would probably not succeed because of the overriding principles described in Chapter 1.

Living accommodation means more than a share of bath-room and/or lavatory. The test of whether or not something is living accommodation is whether the purpose of the room is fulfilled by merely visiting it to perform some function within it. A kitchen is considered to be living accommodation, because kitchens have traditionally been used for more than merely cooking in, *i.e.* many people have customarily used kitchens both to eat in and, indeed, to sit around in. An actual living-room is, obviously, living accommodation. A mere share of cooking facilities, however, *e.g.* if there is a cooker in a hall-way, would not qualify.

This issue is extremely unlikely to arise in connection with a tenancy commencing after August 14, 1974, because it could only apply to a situation in which, on the one hand, the land-lord used the premises, but, on the other, he did not establish sufficient residence to qualify as a resident landlord. It may, however, be relevant to an argument over whether or not the tenant was protected at the beginning of the tenancy if the landlord took up residence shortly before August 14, 1974 and is trying to establish that the tenancy was not protected then. The fact that a tenant is sharing living accommodation with other tenants only does not affect protection at all.

(iv) *Attendances*

A tenancy will be a protected tenancy unless the tenant is, under the terms of the tenancy, provided with attendances, and the value to the tenant of the attendances forms a substan-tial proportion of the whole rent. The substantiality test is identical to that applicable to the question of furniture and the same principles will apply, although attendances may be some-what harder to value.

Attendance means some personal service performed, in the premises in question, for the tenant, for example room clean-ing, changing the sheets, doing the tenant's laundry, etc. It does not include provision of gas or electricity, or hot water, nor does it include cleaning of the common parts of a house in multiple occupation, *e.g.* hallways, stairs, bathroom, lavatory, etc. The provision of a resident housekeeper does not mean that of definition the tenant is provided with attendances, but this is likely to be the case. The full amount of the wages of the resident housekeeper should not be attributed to the tenants, as a whole, even if apportioned between them, for the presence of a resident housekeeper is considered to be of value also to the landlord. Window-cleaning is another service which is considered to be partly of value to the landlord and partly an attendance upon the tenant.

All tenants excluded from protection for one of the reasons described above will be subject to the jurisdiction of the Rent Tribunal: Chapter 5.

(v) *Board*

Any tenant who, under the terms of his tenancy, is provided with any amount of board cannot be a protected tenant. Board means more than a mere morning cup of tea and it is thought that it will mean more than the provision of pre-packaged foods, as described in Chapter 1, although this issue has yet to be tested in the courts. Board traditionally means meals, rather than merely food, of the sort provided in lodgings or boarding-houses, i.e. at least one full, cooked meal each day.

(vi) *Low Rent*

The Act is not designed to catch those who purchase long leases and pay only a small, annual ground rent. These, of course, have been considered as owner-occupiers and were dealt with in Chapter 3. The annual ground rent will be less than two-thirds of the rateable value of the premises and as such the letting is excluded from protection by this "low rent" provision. A low rent is one which is less than two-thirds of the rateable value. However, there is one important exception to this: because of the increases in rateable values in recent years, controlled tenants are almost invariably paying a rent which is less than two-thirds of the rateable value of the premises they occupy. This provision, therefore, does not apply to controlled tenancies at all.

(vii) *Student Lettings*

A tenancy will not be a protected tenancy if the landlord under the tenancy is a specified educational institution *and* the tenant is following or intends to follow a course of study at that or another specified educational institution. Some such institutions, *e.g.* universities, have used this exemption to provide more accommodation to their own students. The university takes a tenancy of premises which are privately owned and, with consent, sublets them to students. Because the university is not a "natural being," at the termination of the tenancy it cannot lay claim to a statutory tenancy (see 2, below) and the student subtenant will not become the landlord's tenant directly because he will not have been a protected subtenant, as a result of this exemption: see also, *Subtenants*, Chapter 2.

Tenants who are excluded from protection for any one of the last three reasons described above may come within the jurisdiction of the Rent Tribunal: see Chapter 5.

(viii) *No Rent*

If no rent is paid under the terms of the tenancy, the tenancy cannot be protected. This is because Rent Act jurisdiction over tenancies has always dealt primarily in the protection of rents, and only secondarily in the protection of rights of occupation. It has been decided that rent must mean payment of rent in money if the tenancy is to be brought within protection, *i.e.* not payment in goods or services. However, there is some authority for the proposition that if the goods or services represent a quantified or agreed sum of money which would otherwise be payable by way of rent, the Act may apply, *i.e.* the tenancy may be protected (*Barnes* v. *Barratt*). Certainly, where an amount of rent between a landlord/employer and his tenant/employee has been agreed but is deducted at source, it is extremely likely that this will be considered sufficient payment of rent for the purposes of protection.

(ix) *Holiday Lettings*

If the purpose of the tenancy was for use as a holiday home, then the tenancy will not be protected. This is another exemption which has been widely used as a device to defeat the Rent Acts. The mere fact that someone has been compelled to sign an agreement alleging falsely that the tenancy was for a holiday purpose does not make it so as a matter of law. On the one hand, the principles described in Chapter 1 will apply to determine whether the agreement was a mere device to exclude protection; on the other hand, occupiers should be aware that once they have signed such an agreement, the courts will consider that the burden of proof is upon them to displace the inference that the tenancy is not protected (*Buchmann* v. *May*). If, therefore, a tenant is contemplating signing such an agreement, with the intention of subsequently seeking a declaration that it is a mere sham, he would be well-advised to stack up as much evidence as he can that the landlord was well aware by the time the agreement was signed that the tenant was not on holiday and did not require the premises for a holiday purpose, for example by telling the landlord so in front of a witness who will be prepared later to testify as to what was said. What is a holiday is a question of fact and common sense.

(x) *Identity of Landlord*

The tenants of the following landlords will not be protected: local authorities, New Town authorities, the Crown, a government department, Registered Housing Associations, Housing Trusts, The Housing Corporation, a housing co-operative. If premises are purchased by one of these bodies, then the tenancy will cease to be protected and will be subject only to the normal rules regulating their tenants; see Chapter 6.

(xi) *Rateable Value*

Some premises have such a high rateable value that they are considered to be the sorts of accommodation which are beyond the scope of protection, *i.e.* because they provide accommodation for the very wealthy. It is the part of the premises which the tenant occupies which must be valued, not the whole house in which the tenancy is situated. A block of flats will often, as a whole, have too high a rateable value for Rent Act purposes, but each individual flat will not. A tenancy will not be a protected tenancy if the premises have a rateable value in excess of £1,500 (Greater London) or £750 (elsewhere). This is so unlikely to be the case that it is quite safe to assume that it is not unless the contrary is proved by the landlord.

None of the tenancies excluded from protection by one of the last three reasons referred to above will fall within the jurisdiction of the Rent Tribunal. They are, therefore, considered in Chapter 6.

Despite this extensive list of exemptions, the majority of private tenancies in this country are fully protected and, as such, subject to the rights of occupation and rent regulation, which we shall now turn to consider.

2. *Security of Tenure*

As has already been remarked (Chapter 2), no tenant can be evicted, whether lawfully in fact or by court proceedings, so long as the tenancy has not been brought to an end. In the case of a protected tenant, this means the contractual tenancy. The contractual tenancy may have come to an end by expiry of a fixed-term, by notice to quit that complies with the conditions described, or by forfeiture. It is unlikely to have come to an end by surrender, if the tenant is still living in the premises. In addition, there are circumstances in which a landlord can serve a notice of increase of rent which has the same effect as a notice to quit, but which need only comply with some of the conditions of notice to quit. This is considered further, below, under the heading of *Rent Limits*.

Once the contractual tenancy has come to an end, the tenant has an absolute right to continue living in the premises indefinitely and as a statutory tenant on, by and large, the same terms as under the contractual tenancy *until*:

(i) The statutory tenancy itself terminates for want of continued residence; *or*

(ii) The premises become overcrowded in law, or are subject to a closing or demolition order because of their condition; *or*

(iii) The landlord establishes to a court, which will be the county court, that one of the stated sets of circumstances exists, as a result of which he is or may be entitled to an order of the court for possession; *or*

(iv) The premises are bought by one of the public or quasi-public landlords described in 1(x), above and the tenant is removed from protection. The tenancy may subsequently be determined and the tenant rehoused or evicted subject to the conditions described in Chapter 6. This will not be considered further in this chapter.

(i) *Statutory Residence*

The purpose of the Rent Act is to protect homes. It is not designed to provide a sometime tenant with a source of income, through subletting or letting to a number of sharers, through as many tenancies as he can acquire. Once the contractual tenancy has come to an end, a statutory tenancy will only come into and remain in being so long as the tenant is in statutory residence. This is exactly the same degree of residence that a landlord must sustain in order to qualify as a resident landlord. During the contractual tenancy there is no obligation at all upon a tenant to do so much as set foot in the premises, although one who fails to do so may have a hard time later establishing residence during the statutory period.

Statutory residence, for these purposes as for the purposes of resident landlords, must be continual although, again, this does not mean that the tenant must constantly be living in the premises. It means that he must always be able to claim that the premises are still in his use as *a* home, even if not as an only home. If a tenant is absent from premises for a longish period of time, for example at the least a few months, there may on the face of it be a claim that he has abandoned use of the premises as a home. Use as a home means "a substantial degree of regular personal occupation by the tenant of an essentially personal nature" (*Herbert* v. *Byrne*.) A person who is absent for long periods *may* still be using the premises as a home, even if he is also using somewhere else in the same way. The question is whether the tenant is keeping on the premises in question "as a mere convenience" (*Beck* v. *Sholtz*) or whether it is in fact the case that he is actually using both places as homes, even if he only visits one or other of them infrequently.

Regardless of whether a person is laying claim to two homes

or not, a person who absents himself from premises for a long-ish period of time can still claim to be statutory tenant of them so long as he intends to return at some time in the future to use the premises as a home, and leaves in the premises some visible signs of that intention (*Brown* v. *Brash.*) This may be done by leaving belongings or furniture, or even by leaving a friend in occupation to, as it were, "keep the place warm." But simply leaving a friend in occupation without any intention to return himself to live there, will not be sufficient to maintain the claim to be statutory tenant of the premises. There must be both: intention to return, and some indication of it.

Neither a company nor any other "artificial" body can lay claim to residence (*Reidy* v. *Walker*), and one cannot claim to occupy through an agent. However, a tenant can be treated as still in occupation, even although he has no intention to return, if he leaves his spouse living in the premises (*Wabe* v. *Taylor.*) This can only last so long as the marriage lasts and will therefore cease to apply on decree absolute. A non-tenant abandoned spouse should take steps to have the tenancy trans-ferred into his name before divorce proceedings are con-cluded: see Chapter 9.

Strictly, once the statutory residence ceases, the statutory tenancy comes automatically to an end. However, the possibi-lities of a mistake being made, especially on the subject of abandonment, and especially by a landlord who may be a little too eager to reclaim the premises, are so high that most land-lords will in fact commence proceedings for a court order for possession before taking the premises back over. Court pro-ceedings are dealt with in Appendix 1.

(ii) *Overcrowding and closing orders*

Even if statutory residence can be sustained, and even if the contractual tenancy has not been brought to an end, the Rent Act will not apply to premises which are subject to a closing or demolition order because they are unfit, or to premises which are being occupied by so many people that they are statutorily overcrowded. Overcrowding is described below, but closing and demolition orders are dealt with in the book *Housing: Repairs and Improvements.*

It is an offence to occupy or to permit to be occupied premises which are subject to an order or which are overcrowded. To avoid an offence, a landlord of premises subject to a closing or demolition order must serve a notice to quit, if he is able to do so, but once the contractual tenancy has come to an end, is not obliged to take proceedings to evict the tenant. He cannot be described as permitting premises to be used once he has withdrawn his permission (*i.e.* contractually) simply by failing to take proceedings to evict the tenant. The offence of occupying overcrowded premises occurs once the premises become overcrowded, but that of permitting premises which are overcrowded to be used only arises once a notice has been served by the local authority stating that the premises are overcrowded. If such a notice is served, the landlord is under an obligation to bring the tenancy to an end, if he is able to do so, and to take proceedings for possession. If there is no way of bringing the contractual tenancy to an end, for example because it is fixed term, then the landlord commits no offence.

The tenant may, however, be committing an offence both during and after the contractual tenancy. That offence is of occupying premises which are overcrowded, or of occupying premises subject to a closing or demolition order. Neither offence is frequently prosecuted: in the latter case, because there is a positive obligation on the local authority to rehouse the tenant and it is usually the local authority's delay in fulfilling this obligation that causes the tenant to stay in occupation at all. In the former case slightly different provisions apply.

Overcrowding is defined in the Housing Act 1957. Premises are overcrowded when the number of persons sleeping in the house is *either* such that any two of those persons, being persons 10 years old or more of opposite sexes, and not being persons living together as husband and wife, must sleep in the same room, *or* is, in relation to the number and floor areas of the rooms of which the premises consist, in excess of the permitted number of occupiers as defined in Schedule 6 to the Act (s. 77). Rent books must state the 'permitted number' of occupiers in relation to the premises.

People do not have to be married to be living together as husband and man. A child under one year of age does not count at all, and children under 10 years old count as half a unit. If premises will become overcrowded as a consequence of a child growing up beyond a particular age, *e.g.* turning ten, then provided the tenant applies for rehousing from the local authority before the premises would otherwise become statutorily overcrowded, they are not to be treated as overcrowded unless and until the tenant subsequently refuses an offer of suitable alternative accommodation. Premises are not considered statutorily overcrowded because a member of the tenant's family comes to stay temporarily.

(iii) *Grounds for Possession*

The most usual way for a person who does not voluntarily give up possession of premises subject to a protected tenancy to leave the premises is because a court order for possession against him is made. Court orders are described generally in Appendix 1. There are three sorts of court order: the first sort is an immediate order which can be executed without any period of delay other than that resulting from the time it takes to get a bailiff to evict the occupier. The court will normally only make such an order against a trespasser (see Chap. 6). Secondly, there is what is commonly called an outright order, which is to say that the court has power to grant some finite period of delay, usually four weeks but on occasion, in extreme hardship, sometimes stretched to six weeks. Once the period of delay granted by the court has run out, then the landlord can issue a bailiff's warrant and there may be a further period of delay before any actual eviction. This sort of order will be granted against any former tenant who is not a protected tenant, and in some circumstances it will be granted against even a former protected tenant. It will also apply to former licensees (see Chap. 6). Lastly, there is the suspended order for possession, which may be either an order suspended for a period longer than four or six weeks, or an order suspended indefinitely, but on conditions. This sort of order has already been referred to, in Chapter Three, as the likely consequence of mortgage arrears which can be cleared in a reasonable time. It is also an appropriate order in connection with a protected tenant who is in rent arrears and in some other circumstances relating to former protected tenants.

The way in which a landlord can get a court order for possession is by issuing proceedings against the tenant and proving to the court that one of the *grounds for possession* appropriate to a protected tenant exists. Unless he can do this, the court has no power to make an order for possession. The grounds for possession are divided into two classes: those in which a court *must* make an outright order for possession, and those in which a court *may* either make an outright order, or may make a suspended order, or even may not make any order at all, even although the ground is shown to exist. In this latter class of grounds for possession, it is not merely enough to show that the circumstances described in the Rent Act exist, but also that it is reasonable to make an order. In effect, in the second class of grounds for possession, the court has a generous and broad discretion to do what it thinks is just and equitable in all the circumstances. It serves to prevent an order for possession being made because of, for example, a trivial breach of one of the terms of the tenancy, or even an outright breach of what the court considers an unnecessary or onerous term, or perhaps because, although a serious breach has occurred, the court is satisfied that it will not be repeated.

Not all tenants who are threatened with court proceedings remain in possession until an order is made. Courts are, after all, only there to resolve disputes. It is within the bounds of possibility that a tenant will agree that a breach is so serious that the court is going to make an outright order and so chose to depart, without running up any liability to legal costs. Or else the tenant may be so seriously in arrears, that he would rather leave before a court judgment for the amount in question is made and he becomes not only homeless but also liable to a larger debt. Landlords rarely pursue a claim for rent arrears alone, once a tenant has left. When a tenant is confronted by the likelihood of action, and perhaps turns to his social worker for advice, it is as well to bear in mind the provisions of the Housing (Homeless Persons) Act 1977, and in particular, the definition of intentional homelessness, which effectively removes the right to full rehousing, contained therein (see Chap. 10).

The circumstances in which a court *must* make an order for possession are those set out in Part 2, Schedule 15, to the Rent

Act 1977. For example, a landlord who formerly occupied premises as his home can reclaim possession from a protected tenant because he wants to live there again, provided certain notice qualifications are fulfilled. Similarly, a landlord who buys a house for his retirement can also secure a possession order against a protected tenant when the time has come for retirement, again subject to notice qualifications. There are some miscellaneous grounds dealing with premises occupied in connection with religion or agriculture. There are also two grounds which relate to out-of-season lettings of premises normally subject to a holiday tenancy, and premises normally let out to students. In each case, during the off-season, or during a year when there is not the normal demand for student accommodation, the landlord can let out the premises on a protected tenancy and yet reclaim them when he wants them back. The conditions for the operation of these grounds are extremely tightly defined, so as to avoid abuse.

The circumstances in which a court *may* make an order for possession are those set out in s. 98 and Part 1 of Schedule 15, to the Rent Act 1977. It is when a landlord reclaims possession on one of these grounds that he must also establish to the court that it is reasonable to make the order, and when an order is made on one of these grounds that the court has a discretion to make a suspended order, *e.g.* for possession suspended so long as the tenant pays the current rent plus an amount each week off the arrears, or possession suspended so long as the tenant does not commit a further nuisance or annoyance to neighbours, or so long as the tenant repairs some damage or repairs or replaces some item of furniture which has been harmed by his default. In the main, these grounds are ones where the tenant has been in some default, for example, the tenant or someone living with him has been a nuisance or annoyance to neighbours (not including the landlord, unless he happens to be a neighbour); the tenant or someone living with him has used the premises for an illegal or immoral purpose; the tenant or someone living with him has damaged the premises or furniture provided under the terms of the letting; the tenant is in breach of the terms of the tenancy; the tenant is in arrears of rent. It is quite common for a landlord to forget, when using one of these grounds for possession, that he must also terminate a periodic tenancy which is still contractual.

In addition, there are grounds which deal with a tenant of premises also used as an off-licence, and a ground for possession which arises if the tenant has a subtenant and the tenant is overcharging the subtenant on a fair (see 3, below) or registered (see Chap. 5) rent. If a tenant gives notice to quit, in consequence of which the landlord contracts to sell or relet the premises, or otherwise acts to his disadvantage, he will be able to claim possession against the tenant, but for this ground to apply it is essential that the notice to quit should be a technically valid notice. It does not apply to a purported surrender. The landlord can also reclaim possession from the tenant if, after certain dates contained in the Schedule, the tenant sublets the whole of the premises, whether at one time or bit by bit, or assigns the tenancy. This is so even if there is no prohibition in the tenancy agreement preventing subletting or assignment. This ground underlines the idea that a statutory tenant holds on the same terms as the contractual tenancy, so long as they are consistent with statutory tenancy, and that the purpose of the statutory tenancy is to provide the right to use premises as a home, not for making a profit out of them.

The courts are not reluctant to use the power to suspend an order. It will be the usual result of a case of arrears of rent which are not too serious, or where there is no long history of bad payment, or other breaches of the tenancy which are not irremediable, immitigable or inexcusably serious. It may be that the court is inclined to make a full order when it finds that a serious nuisance or annoyance has been caused, or where the arrears are very high indeed. A social worker may well be in a position to make representations to the court that there is scope for a suspended order by explaining the cause of the arrears, or the circumstances leading to the nuisance or annoyance, *e.g.* emotional disturbance, with sufficient force to persuade the court to give the tenant a further chance.

There are three cases in which there is no default at all on the part of the tenant. In one of them, there is an element of caution that the tenancy may be terminable. Service tenants may be evicted on a special ground which applies only to them: that the premises are reasonably required for use as a residence by another person who is in the landlord's employment, or who would be but for the want of premises. There has to be a particular new service tenant in mind, and the landlord and the employer must be exactly the same person in law, see p. 40). It must also be reasonable to make the order.

The second such case is where the landlord requires the premises for use as a residence for himself or one of a specified list of members of his family, *e.g.* his parents, or a child over the age of 18. The landlord cannot use this ground if he bought the premises subject to the tenancy, and it is still necessary to show that it would be reasonable to make the order. There is a special defence to such an action: if the tenant can show that, in all the circumstances, particularly having regard to the availability of other accommodation to either landlord or tenant, greater hardship would be caused by granting the order than by refusing it, the court will not make an order at all.

The courts do not like this ground for possession because, once it is established that the need of the landlord is genuine, they are called upon to make a very difficult decision indeed. A landlord may, however, have this important advantage over the tenant: he may at least own the premises in question and, if they are not already subject to a mortgage, may be able to raise money with which to buy somewhere else for himself or the member of the family in question. The courts should also be reminded that the landlord has been taking advantage of the property by drawing rent out of it for, perhaps, several years and it will be appropriate to examine the landlord as to what has been done with this money. This case is often used when the landlord's own home has been compulsorily purchased: see Chapter 7. In such circumstances, the local authority for the area of the other property is obliged to provide the landlord with alternative accommodation if he has nowhere suitable already. If the court refuses to make an order against the tenant, the landlord may still be able to go back to that authority and ask for rehousing.

On the other hand, if the tenant falls within the category of people to be treated as having a priority need for rehousing when homeless, then the tenant will be rehoused by the local authority and the court will be more inclined to make the order: see Chapter 10. If the order is refused, the landlord himself may be homeless and have a priority need, in which case the balance of hardship will probably tip in favour of the tenant and no order should be made.

Lastly, this is a ground for possession which is frequently abused and it may be, for example, that the landlord has already made plans to sell the property with vacant possession. This may be shown up by enquiries at local estate agents for property in the area, and if the property is included on such a list, the landlord will stand very little chance indeed of regaining possession and may, indeed, be in serious trouble for attempting to deceive the court.

If an order for possession is made under this last ground, or the one before, that which is appropriate to service tenants, and it is later made to appear to the court that the landlord obtained the order either by misrepresenting circumstances to the court, or by concealing some material fact, the court has power to make the landlord pay substantial damages to the tenant: Rent Act 1977, s. 102. This is a difficult claim, because it will not be enough to show, for example, that the premises have subsequently been put up for sale. It must be shown that there was active misrepresentation at the time of the court hearing. Any order obtained by fraud can always be set aside but, because this is an allegation of a criminal offence, it must be proved beyond reasonable doubt even in a civil court, which can be very hard to do.

The most common ground for possession of all those discussed here is that the landlord can provide or obtain suitable alternative accommodation for the tenant. As with most of the grounds under discussion, the schedule to Part 4 contains details as to exactly what the landlord must prove. In the case of suitable alternative accommodation, the landlord may be able to establish his claim by producing a certificate from the local authority that the tenant will be rehoused by them. In the alternative, a landlord can himself provide another private tenancy or obtain one for the tenant from another landlord. In this case, the Schedule regulates such details as suitability for the needs and means of the tenant and his family as regards extent and character; or its similarity to the existing accommodation; and also the extent of protection that the tenant will enjoy. Alternative accommodation will never be suitable if it will result in overcrowding, even if the tenant's present premises are overcrowded. Suitable alternative accommodation may consist of part only of a tenant's present premises, for example, if one room is sublet or disused. But if the part of the premises which the landlord is seeking to recover is used at all, for example, as a study or workroom, or a spare room for visiting family, it is extremely unlikely that the court will allow this ground for possession to be used, effectively, to reduce the size of the tenancy.

The landlord must still establish that it is reasonable to make the order. A court will frequently refuse, even where the alternative premises are ostensibly eminently suitable, because of, for example, the age of the tenant. An order may well be made subject to undertakings from the landlord to do specific works to the new premises, or else to pay for various removal expenses, etc. If such undertakings are not fulfilled, the tenant can apply to the court to set aside or discharge the order, or sue for the amount owing. The character of the new premises can be a determining factor. In *Redspring* v. *Francis*, it was held that premises on a busy road next door to a fish and chip shop, were not suitable for a tenant who had hitherto been living in a quiet residential street. The extent of the facilities and amenities in an area, including shops, open space, transport, etc., will also influence a decision.

In any of the circumstances in which a court makes an order suspended on terms or conditions, it is well worthwhile for the tenant to reapply to the court to discharge the order, once the term or condition of the suspension has been fulfilled, for example because all the arrears have been paid off. It is undesirable to leave on the court file a possession order which a landlord may subsequently be able to reactivate with little or no notice, perhaps because the tenant falls slightly, even accidentally, into arrears at some later date (see Appendix 1).

3. *Protection of Rents*

All protected tenants, whether statutory or contractual, controlled or regulated, are entitled to protection of their rents. Indeed, statutory tenancy itself would be valueless if landlords could increase rents beyond what tenants can afford to pay, and so force them speedily into arrears. The converse is equally true: protection of rents would be valueless if landlords could serve retaliatory notices to quit, as, indeed, almost always happens to a restricted tenant who seeks registration of rent with the Rent Tribunal (see Chapter 5.)

Controlled tenants pay controlled rents. Regulated tenants need only pay fair rents. Rent protection, like much of housing law, is extremely complex and often highly technical. It, too, involves consideration of whether or not a tenancy is still contractual for in some circumstances the contractual rent can form the rent limit, even where a fair rent has been registered which is higher. In this section we shall consider:

(i) What the fair rent is;
(ii) How it applies to a tenancy;
(iii) The rent limit for regulated tenancies; and
(iv) Controlled rents.

(i) *The fair rent*

A fair rent is one that is considered fair for the premises and tenancy in question by a Rent Officer. He is a public official, employed by the Department of the Environment through a series of local Rent Offices throughout the country. Each Rent Office has jurisdiction over an area broadly corresponding to an area of local government.

The Rent Act contains guidelines to Rent Officers as to what they should consider as a fair rent. There are some things which they are obliged to take into account, and some which they are bound to disregard. Failure to obey these guidelines could result in an application to the Divisional Court to quash the decision of the Rent Officer. It is, however, hard to establish that a Rent Officer has either wrongly taken account of some factor, or else failed to apply some relevant consideration.

The Rent Officer is obliged to take into account all the circumstances (other than personal circumstances) and in particular the age, character, and locality of the residential accommodation, its state of repair, and if any furniture is provided for use under the tenancy the quantity, quality and condition of the furniture (Rent Act 1977, s. 70.)

The most common example of a personal circumstance is the tenant who is in straitened circumstances, or the landlord who claims that he cannot afford to keep the property in repair. Another example might be that of an elderly person who finds it more inconvenient to live at the top of a flight of stairs than would a hypothetical, average tenant; or a tenant with children who feels the lack of a garden. But the presence or otherwise of a garden, and the fact that a flat is at the top of, perhaps, a long flight of stairs, will affect the premises themselves in any event, just not more so because of the particular characteristics or circumstances of the present tenant.

Although it is not permissible to take into account the tenant's financial circumstances, it is possible for a Rent Officer to consider the general level of wages throughout a particular locality (*Guppy's (Bridport) Ltd.* v. *Carpenter*). But it is up to the Rent Officer to determine just what he will consider the locality for the purposes of the determination (*Palmer* v. *Peabody Trust.*) This could benefit a tenant of whatever income living in a working class district but, equally, could act to the detriment of a poor tenant living in an area that is, or has become, predominantly middle class.

Such matters as size and whether or not premises are on a noisy street are obviously relevant. Consideration of locality means more than just what part of town premises are in, but also whether they are near other amenities, such as parks and recreational facilities, public transport and good shopping centres. In other words, all the factors you would normally consider as affecting the value of living in particular premises. State of repair is very important indeed; if premises are in such a bad condition that they are not even habitable, or perhaps only in part habitable, then there is nothing to stop a Rent Officer determining a purely nominal rent for the premises as a whole, or attributing a purely nominal amount to the uninhabitable part (*McGee* v. *London Borough of Hackney*).

The Rent Officer will disregard, in addition to personal circumstances, any improvements done by the tenant, other than improvements which he is obliged to do under the terms of the tenancy, and any damage or disrepair attributable to the tenant's default. He will also disregard certain, recent local amenities which have been paid for out of public funds.

The major element which the Rent Officer must disregard, that forms the cornerstone of the fair rent system, is the "scarcity value." It is scarcity, more than anything else, which pushes up the price of property and rents. It is easy to see how a landlord with considerable property holdings in a particular area could manipulate the supply of property and, accordingly, its relationship to demand, without difficulty. In order to avoid scarcity value, the Rent Officer is obliged to adopt the artificial assumption that there are not noticeably more people seeking any particular sort of accommodation in one area, than there is such accommodation available.

Each Rent Office is obliged to maintain a rent register, which is open for public inspection. This contains details of all rent registrations in force. Normally these are rents which will have been registered by a Rent Officer since 1965, when the fair rent system was introduced. There is one exception to this. Prior to August 14, 1974, furnished tenancies were subject to the Rent Tribunal (see 1, above) and rents may have been registered in respect of them with the Rent Tribunal (see Chapter 5.) When the Rent Act 1974 came into force, such rent registrations were deemed to become fair rents and were included in the register.

The rent register contains the documentary part of the experience which the Rent Officer will apply to any particular application. He will look at the register to see if there have been any previous registrations for properties of similar size, in similar areas, etc. These, the Rent Officer will treat as "comparables." Comparables are very important indeed and anyone considering an application for registration of a fair rent should take the trouble to go down to the Rent Office and inspect the register, which is open to the public.

It is important to note the date of a comparable for, like everything else, rents increase with inflation and the cost of living generally. Rents are always registered exclusive of rates and many tenants will in fact be paying a rent that is inclusive, so that without bearing this in mind a comparable can be deceptively encouraging. They can be misleading for another reason; while the register gives details of any special facilities provided under the terms of the tenancy, such as services or

furniture, and attributes how much of the rent is paid for
them, and while the register also indicates the balance of
repairing obligations as between landlord and tenant, the
register will rarely include any or much information about the
state of the property which is being considered comparable.
Clearly it would not be fair for a tenant to pay as much for
property in bad condition as for one in a good state of repair.
It may even be worth calling round to the other property and
noting any differences in condition or, indeed, other matters
which have not shown up on the register.

(ii) *Application of fair rents*

A fair rent can apply to a tenancy in one of two ways; either
there is a rent already registered, or there is an application for
a registration after the tenancy starts.

If there has been a registration before the tenancy starts,
then this rent will apply to the new tenancy, even though the
tenancy agreement is for a higher figure. A fair rent applies to
any subsequent tenancy, unless and until such time as a new
application is made. The only exception to this is that a rent
registered at a time when the premises were unfurnished will
not apply to a subsequent letting which is furnished in law (see
1(i), above), even though that later tenancy is protected (see
Metrobarn v. *Gehring*). The rent only applies, however, to
exactly the same premises, *i.e.* not premises which have been
enlarged by the addition of a room, nor even premises reduced
in size by letting them off less one of the rooms. A fair rent only
applies to subsequent regulated tenancies.

There is one, exceptional way in which a fair rent can be
removed from the register, without any new application. This
applies in very limited circumstances indeed. If a landlord and
a tenant under a fixed term tenancy on which there is at least
one year to run agree on a higher rent, they may apply to the
Rent Officer to remove the registration of a fair rent, which
will be done provided that the Rent Officer approves the
amount of the increase. This can only be done at least three
years after the last registration and it is so uncommon that it
will not be considered further here.

If a tenant has been paying more than the registered rent,

under a contract, then the excess if recoverable, for up to two years after it was paid, either by deducting it from future rent owing, or by a normal civil action: (see Appendix 1). It is necessary to be very sure that the tenant has been paying a higher rent, for it is likely that the later rent was inclusive of rates, while the registration is exclusive. To work out whether a higher than fair rent is being charged, it is necessary to calculate the rates due for the premises, or part of the premises occupied by the tenant, and add them to the fair rent. If the figure produced is still lower than the contractual rent, there has been an overpayment. If it is higher, then the contractual rent will apply (see (iii), below). If both rents, registered and contractual, are exclusive of rates, then it is only necessary to compare the two exclusive rents.

There can only be an application for a new registration, in normal circumstances, three years after the last. This is so even if there is a new tenancy or, indeed, even if there is a new landlord, so that two completely different parties could find themselves bound by a registration secured by a former landlord and/or a former tenant. Either landlord, or tenant, or both jointly, or a local authority can apply for registration of rent. The local authority has power to do this along with various other powers concerning private rented accommodation in its area, *e.g.* housing conditions (see *Housing: Repairs and Improvements*), harassment and illegal eviction (see Chap. 8) and other landlord/tenant offences described throughout this book. It may choose to exercise this power because, for example, in connection with the rent allowance scheme (see Chapter 7), it wishes to rationalise rents throughout its area, or else because it is seeking to avert any possible hostility from the landlord if the tenant were to apply on his own. A social worker should not hesitate to ask the local authority to use this power if he is working with a client who is likely to be intimidated from or inhibited about making an application. The local authority power exists whether the application is the first ever application, or a new application after the three year delay.

There are three exceptions to the three-year bar:

(a) where a landlord and a tenant apply jointly for a new rent to be registered, this may be done in less than three years;

(b) a landlord may apply on his own, two years and 9 months after the last registration, but the new rent cannot come into force until three years have elapsed; and

(c) if there have been such substantial changes in the terms of the tenancy, the condition of the premises or furniture, that, in all the circumstances, the rent last registered is no longer fair, then either party can apply for a new rent to be registered in less than three years. On such an application, the Rent Officer does not merely consider the changed circumstances and reduce or increase accordingly, but considers the whole rent anew. This provision is likely only to be of use to a landlord who has, for example, installed some new facility such as a new hot water system, since the last registration. A tenant who applies because of some deterioration may well find that the amount by which the rent ought to be decreased on account of the deterioration is not so great as the amount by which the rent has increased in respect of the rent of the tenancy, because of inflation. On the other hand, on a landlord's application for a higher rent because of an improvement, a tenant should not hesitate to point out any deterioration, so as to prevent the rent going up by too much.

If there is no rent already in force, the tenant can apply at any time after the start of a tenancy, even if it is a matter of days since he signed an agreement to pay a particular rent which he considers too high. Tenants' general willingness to sign anything in order to get a roof over their heads has already been referred to in Chapter 1; they need not be inhibited about immediately going back on an agreement by application for a fair rent, for it is exactly this sort of difficulty from which the legislation extricates them.

The procedure is the same, whether or not the application is a first application or a new application. The party making the application completes the appropriate forms, which are available from the Rent Office and from most aid or advice agencies. These forms will be sent to the other side, for example, the landlord on a tenant's application, who will have an opportunity to comment and to put the case from his point of view. If there are joint tenants or, indeed, joint landlords, then all must sign the application form or one must sign as agent for the others, see Chapter 2, Joint Tenants, p. 45. The applicant is obliged to state what is the fair rent that he wishes to have registered.

Although the Rent Officer is not obliged to do so, he will almost invariably visit the premises. He will hold a consultation at the time, or, in some circumstances, back at his office. The consultation is informal and it is not usual for parties to be represented, nor is legal aid available for such representation, although legal advice may be obtained beforehand (see Appendix 2). A lawyer may be of help if a question of jurisdiction arises, for example whether the tenancy is regulated or not, or whether the time is correct for an application. A surveyor may be of more help if the only question is as to the amount of rent. Some Rent Officers give their decision at the hearing, others do so later. In either case, the decision will be in writing. There does not even need to be a consultation if the application is a joint application between landlord and tenant, but the Rent Officer is still bound to consider the amount to be registered, because, of course, it will fix on the premises, not just on the tenancy in question.

If either party is dissatisfied with the rent registration, they may appeal to the Rent Assessment Committee. This body has no power at all to decide an appeal on a point of law, *i.e.* as to jurisdiction. Such an appeal can only be taken to the Divisional Court or to the county court: see Appendix 1. The Rent Assessment Committee is a tribunal, not a court, and legal aid is not available for proceedings before it, although legal advice may be obtained beforehand: see Appendix 2. Again, representation by a surveyor may be helpful. There is a Surveyor's Aid Scheme operating in London for those who cannot afford a surveyor without help.

When the Rent Assessment Committee hears an appeal, it does not start with the decision of the Rent Officer and decide whether there is right or wrong, but starts all over again for itself. It, too, will normally go to inspect the premises in question, and it will always hold a consultation which will be slightly more formal than that before the Rent Officer and will always be at their office, not at the premises. There is no appeal from a joint application to the Rent Officer.

Rent Assessment Committee rents are customarily higher than those of the Rent Officer, by an average of about 10 per cent. There is no explanation for this but it tends to suggest that tenants are rarely well-advised to appeal, unless there is some general point at issue and a case is being laid by way of test-case, or the Rent Officer's decision is clearly unsupportable. There is no appeal from a Rent Assessment Committee decision, unless it can be shown to have acted wrongly in law, by wrongful inclusion or exclusion of some consideration. This would also be made to the Divisional Court.

The date when the registration is finally made, either by Rent Officer or Assessment Committee, is known as the date of registration, and it affects the date when a new application can be made. The date of the application is normally known as the effective date. When either a Rent Officer or a Rent Assessment Committee registers a rent, he or it will do so from the date of application, unless he or it is asked and consents to enter a later date as the effective date. The rent applies to the tenancy from the effective date.
The rent applies to the tenancy from the effective date.

If an application is a first application, it will usually be made by a tenant and it will usually result in a decrease in the rent from that which was agreed contractually. This means that by the time of an actual registration, the landlord has in fact received more rent than is due and the tenant is entitled to recoup the balance, either by civil action or, more usually, by way of deduction from future rent. If the rent registered is higher, taken together with rates if the contractual rent is inclusive, than the contractual rent, then the landlord cannot claim the increase until he has brought the contractual tenancy to an end, either by notice to quit or, in the case of a fixed term tenancy, by expiry of time.

Problems can arise on a new application, or on an appeal to the Rent Assessment Committee. It may be that a contractual rent is agreed at, *e.g.* £20 per week. A fair rent is registered at £10, to which is added the rates of, *e.g.* £2. The landlord is entitled only to £12 per week. Because the rent is lower than the contractual rent, there is no incentive for the landlord to bring the contractual tenancy to an end. If the registration is appealed to the Rent Assessment Committee, or even if the contractual tenancy is still in existence three years later when a new application is made, the rent may increase, and yet remain within the contractual limits. In such a case, the landlord can claim the higher rent without any notice of increase or, indeed, without any phasing provisions applying (see (iii), below.) It follows that far from the landlord owing the tenant money, the tenant may owe the landlord some; this will be the amount of the increase between the effective date and the date of registration on a new application to the Rent Officer, or the amount of the increase between the effective date and the registration date on an appeal to the Rent Assessment Committee. A tenant is, therefore, well advised to put aside some money in the event of an appeal to the Rent Assessment Committee or a new application which takes place during the contractual tenancy, until the decision is known. If the tenancy is already statutory, then a notice of increase will have to be served: see (iii), below.

In addition to the provisions outlined above, a landlord can also apply for what is called a certificate of fair rent. This he can do at a time when there is no tenant in occupation and it applies when a landlord is proposing to carry out work to a property, perhaps converting a house into flats, and wants to know how much he will be able to charge by way of rent once the work has been done. The Rent Officer will visit, and issue a certificate but the certificate will only become effective once the works have been completed and checked. The drawback to this system is that there is no one to, as it were, take the tenant's part and point to the defects and drawbacks of living in the premises.

(iii) *The Rent Limit*

The rent limit is the term used to describe the maximum amount which a landlord can claim from the tenant. It must be considered:

(a) during the contractual period;

(b) after the contractual period, if or when no rent has been registered; and

(c) after the contractual period, once a fair rent has been registered.

(a) Contractual period

During the contractual period of a regulated tenancy, the

rent limit is *either* the registered rent *or* the contractual rent,
whichever is the lower. If there is no registered rent, then the
limit is the contractual rent. The contractual rent may be
inclusive of rates, in which case it will be necessary to add to
the registered rent the amount of rates attributable to the
premises before determining how much rent is payable. Any
increases up to the amount of the contractual limit can be
imposed without notice of increase, and without phasing (see
(c) below) and in order to exceed the contractual limit, the
tenancy must be determined.

(b) Statutory period — pre-registration

It may be that by the time the contractual tenancy comes to
an end, there is still no registered rent in force. In that case,
the landlord is still confined by the former contractual rent
limit, until such time as he applies for registration of a fair
rent. In other words, the landlord cannot normally increase
the rent payable without application. If the result of an
application is an increase, then the landlord must first serve a
notice of increase, and the increase will be phased (see (c)
below.) Once the tenancy is statutory, the tenant need not
worry about new applications or appeals to the Rent Assessment Committee because the landlord cannot recover the full
rent without notice, and phasing, and he cannot serve notice
of increase until he knows to what amount the rent is to be
increased by the Rent Officer or Assessment Committee.

The landlord can, however, increase the rent without
applying for registration, on account of increases in rates payable, and on account of the costs of providing services of
furniture, and in order to reflect a proportion of the amount
spent on improvements to the premises. This does not include
improvement done under grant-aid: see *Housing: Repairs and
Improvements*. In all of these cases, the landlord must serve a
notice of increase, and there are restrictions on how far back
he can claim the increase for. The tenant may be able to
challenge the amount claimed in the county court. These
increases will not be phased (see (c) below.)

One alternative to an increase other than on account of
these items of expenditure and other than by way of application

for registration is for the landlord and the tenant to enter into a rent agreement for a new rent. A rent agreement is only valid if it is in writing, and if at the head of the document there appears a statement in writing or print no less conspicuous than that used elsewhere in the agreement that the tenant is not obliged to enter into the agreement, and that his security of tenure will not be affected if he refuses. The statement must also advise the tenant of his right to apply to the Rent Officer at any time, then or even immediately after it has been signed, for registration of a fair rent. An agreement which does not comply with these terms is invalid and the excess can be reclaimed by the tenant for up to two years after it was paid, as an ordinary civil debt: see Appendix 1.

(c) Statutory period — post-registration

Once a rent is registered for the premises, then this becomes the rent limit and cannot be increased except by a new application, other than to pass on increases in the rates. It is also possible to pass on increases in the cost of providing services without a new application, provided that the Rent Officer has agreed that the services element should be variable and has endorsed the landlord's proposed terms for any future variations, *i.e.* for how they are to be calculated. There can be no increases for other items referred to above.

Increases on account of rates and services do not need to be claimed by way of notice of increase, once the tenancy is statutory and there is a registered rent in existence, and phasing does not apply to them. Other increases, which will be those by new application or, possibly, by appeal to the Rent Assessment Committee, can only be claimed by notice of increase. The period of delay between an application to the Rent Officer and an appeal to the Rent Assessment Committee could make it worth a landlord's while to serve a notice of increase in the meantime, although many do not in fact bother. When a notice of increase has to be served, then the increase is subject to phasing. This means that the full increase is not passed on at once, but is phased over a period of up to three years. A landlord can pass on an increase of one-third of the total increase, or 40p, whichever is the greater, *in any one year*. For example, an increase of 90p would result in an increase of 40p in the first year, 40p in the second, and 10p in the third. But an increase of £1.80 would mean an increase of 60p each year for three years.

With all regulated tenancies, whether contractual or statutory and whether or not a rent is registered in respect of the premises, it is illegal for a landlord to demand rent further in advance than the beginning of the period for which it is paid, *i.e.* the first day of a week for which a weekly rent is paid, or the first day of a month for which a monthly rent is paid. If the tenancy is yearly, then the landlord cannot charge the year's rent earlier than half-way through the year for which it is due. A tenant can recover any money improperly demanded too far in advance, for up to two years after it was paid. This probably does not mean that the landlord is not entitled to the actual rent at the time when it would be lawful to ask for it, so that this would probably only be of any use to a tenant who has been charged a considerable amount in advance, or by way of defence to an action for arrears, or part of them, based on rent improperly charged in advance, *i.e.* because it is, in law, not yet due and therefore not in arrears.

(iv) *Controlled Rents*

Unlike the regulated rent, the controlled rent does apply automatically to a tenancy and it requires neither application to nor the decision of an official to bring it into force. Controlled rents remain in force until the tenancy expires, *i.e.* because of death of the tenant leaving no successor, or departure of the tenant, or until it is converted to regulation. There are provisions for phasing an increase on conversion and the rent allowable on conversion would be either as agreed by rent agreement (see (iii) above), or as registered by the Rent Officer.

It is not necessary to consider the position of the contractual controlled tenant. Because of the qualifications for controlled tenancies, the last one would have had to have been created by July 6, 1957, and not be a tenancy for more than 21 years. Any fixed term controlled tenancy would, therefore, have ended by July 5, 1978. In practice most controlled tenancies are and were periodic in any event. In theory, there could still be a contractual periodic controlled tenancy in existence, but this would mean that no increase, not even on account of rates, had ever been passed on since the start of the tenancy and is so unlikely that the law presumes that a controlled tenancy is statutory unless the tenant can prove the contrary. The controlled rent remains the rent limit throughout, subject to the variations described in the next paragraph.

The controlled rent is one that is calculated as an appropriate factor of the gross value of the dwelling-house as shown in the valuation list of November 7, 1956, to which can be added any rates borne by the landlord, a reasonable charge for services or furniture provided under the terms of the tenancy, and an amount in respect of repairs and improvements. These latter amounts can, obviously, vary and the details for determining just how much of such expenditure the tenant must pay are contained in the Rent Act 1977. In view of their complexity, and in view of the few tenancies affected, it is not proposed to describe these here and they are matters on which qualified advice should be sought.

The appropriate factor varies according to liability for repairs. If the tenant is responsible for repairs, then the basic figure is four-thirds of the gross value; if the tenant is responsible for some but not all of the repairs, then the appropriate factor is to be agreed between the parties or, in default of agreement, by the county court, at a figure of not less than four-thirds and not more than twice the gross value; if the landlord is responsible for all repairs, the appropriate factor is twice the gross value. If a local authority issues a certificate of disrepair, then for the time that it is in force, the appropriate factor drops automatically to four-thirds.

4. *Further Financial Protection*

To avoid other forms of exploitation of tenants, or ways of extracting more money from them than rent regulation and control permit, there are other forms of financial protection which apply to protected (and, in some cases, other) tenancies:

    (i) Premiums and deposits;

    (ii) Accommodation agency charges; and

    (iii) Resale of utilities, *i.e.* gas and electricity.

(i) *Premiums and Deposits*

It is illegal to charge a tenant a premium on the grant, continuance or renewal of a protected tenancy. A tenant who has paid one such premium can sue for its return. Such a claim must be made within six years of the payment in the same way as for the recovery of a normal civil debt: see Appendix 1. It is also a criminal offence to require or to receive a premium and the matter should be reported to the Tenancy Relations or Harassment Officer: see Chapter 8.

A premium might be charged by a landlord, or by his agent, or by an outgoing tenant. An outgoing tenant might charge for an assignment, or else for arranging to surrender his own tenancy to the landlord, who contemporaneously consents to grant a new tenancy to the incoming tenant. In such a case, it may well be that there is no profit to the landlord. In all of these cases, however, the premium is an illegal payment. It is a premium whether a person demands that the money is paid to himself, or to someone else, perhaps, for example in discharge of a debt that the person demanding the premium owes to the other. Another example would be that of the outgoing tenant who agrees to assign the tenancy or arrange for a new tenancy to be granted to the incoming tenant, if the incoming tenant will pay arrears of rent that he owes.

The most obvious form that a premium will take is cash. But an illegal premium might also be demanded or paid other than in cash, for otherwise this protection too could be circumvented without difficulty, *e.g.* by demanding payments in kind, such as goods, or else by demanding excessive prices for fixtures, fittings or furniture. It is lawful to make it a condition of the grant of a tenancy, whether by assignment or from the landlord, that an incoming tenant should have to purchase fittings, or even furniture. After all, such items as fitted carpets may well be valueless to an outgoing tenant in his new home and it seems only fair that he should be able to insist, before the assignment or an arrangement for surrender and new grant, that the incoming tenant, as it were, takes them off his hands. But only a fair price for fittings and furniture can be demanded and the excess constitutes an illegal premium. Anyone seeking to make an incoming tenant pay for furniture is obliged to provide an inventory of it and of the prices sought for each item, and failure to do so is a criminal offence.

The position is slightly different where "fixtures" are concerned. These are items, such as fitted cupboards or double glazing, which effectively become a part of the premises and are meaningless when removed. No tenant is allowed to remove fixtures in any event: as they attach to the premises, then they become, eventually, the property of the landlord. But an outgoing tenant is permitted to charge an incoming tenant the amount it cost him to instal the fixtures. An outgoing tenant is also permitted to charge what it cost him to do any structural alterations to the premises, any amounts paid by way of outgoings on the premises, *e.g.* rates, telephone rental, which are attributable to the period after he has left, and any amount paid by the outgoing tenant to a former tenant which was payment for fixtures or alterations.

Another way of attempting to secure a benefit, usually demanded by a landlord or, on the landlord's behalf, by an agent, is to compel an incoming occupier to pay a deposit, either for furniture, for rent arrears or, for example, damage. It is well-established, and defined in the Act (s. 119), that a demand for a loan constitutes an illegal premium and by analogy, there have been a number of decisions which have ruled that such deposits are also illegal. The intention of Parliament was both to deny a landlord any benefit in addition to lawful rent and also to ensure that incoming tenants would not have to find sums of money which they could not afford. The decisions relating to deposits are, however, lower court decisions and the question has yet to be considered by one of the higher courts. In one of the lower court decisions, it was decided that the deposit did not amount to an illegal premium: in that case, the amount received was placed with a Building Society, the interest accruing to the tenant, and held there for the tenant's benefit. Even this decision seems to contravene the intention not to make people pay out more than rent for their accommodation, but clearly the court was influenced by the lack of benefit to the landlord and the careful, even meticulous way in which it had all been arranged.

(ii) *Accommodation Agency Charges*

Under the Accommodation Agencies Act 1953, it is a criminal offence to demand or to accept any payment either for registering or undertaking to register the name and requirements of a person seeking a tenancy of premises. It is also an offence under the same Act to demand or accept a payment simply for supplying or undertaking to supply addresses or other particulars of premises to let. As well as constituting offences, such payments can be recovered as civil debts within six years of the payment being made: see Appendix 1.

The first provision, registration of requirements, is comparatively straightforward. The second provision has recently been considered by the House of Lords, in the case of *Saunders* v. *Soper*. It was held that the purpose of the provision was to prohibit payments made simply for supplying addresses and particulars of property to let. It does not prohibit payment for actually finding somewhere for the prospective tenant to live. It follows that an illegal payment has been made, and is therefore recoverable by the tenant, if the payment is made simply for the provision of addresses, and also if the payment is made for the provision of addresses, even though expressed to be returnable if the tenant does not accept a tenancy through the services of the agency. The payment is not illegal if made *after* a tenancy has been found and accepted.

(iii) *Resale of Utilities*

Another way in which rent control and the prohibition on premiums could be defeated would be if there was no maximum amount which a landlord could charge for such essential services as gas and electricity. The Electricity Board are entitled to publish a tariff, which may differ from area to area, indicating the maximum amounts which may be charged for the resale of electricity. This will usually be a figure that permits the landlord a small profit per unit, to cover, among other things, the cost of renting the electricity meter which monitors the occupier's use. The Gas Board are under a duty to fix such maximum prices. It is a little surprising that one board should be obliged to do so, while the other is only empowered to do so, but the Electricity Boards do in fact publish such tariffs and if they were to fail to do, no doubt Parliament would reconsider the discretion. In either case, the amounts overcharged are recoverable by the occupier as a civil debt: see Appendix 1.

Further Reading

"A Note on Attendances (and board)," March 1975 LAG Bulletin 73.

"Casereport," April 1975 LAG Bulletin 101.

"A Note on Statutory Residence," December 1974 LAG Bulletin 302.

"Premises Required for Landlord," January 1978 LAG Bulletin 10.

"Suitable Alternative Accommodation," December 1976 LAG Bulletin 280.

"Rents — Some General Principles," October 1976 LAG Bulletin 225.

"Premiums," October 1975 LAG Bulletin 263.

5 Restricted Security

The Rent Tribunal is an official body which has power, where certain types of letting have been granted, to register a reasonable rent for the letting, and to defer for up to six months at a time a notice bringing the letting to an end. Its jurisdiction is over what can only be described as an odd mixture of lettings, some of them tenancies (restricted tenancies) and some of the licences (restricted licences.) Tenancies which are neither protected nor restricted (unrestricted tenancies) and licences which are not restricted (unrestricted licences) are described in Chapter 6. The term "unprotected *tenancy*" applies to all those tenancies which are not *protected, i.e.* it refers to restricted and to unrestricted tenancies.

Although the powers of the Rent Tribunal are defined principally with registration of rent in mind, applications are most commonly made either where a notice has already been served or else the occupier does not mind that the application is likely to result in a retaliatory notice to go. It has been described in Chapter 1 as a commonplace of housing advice that a restricted occupier who applies for registration of rent will indeed receive such a retaliatory notice. The security of tenure available from the Rent Tribunal is not indefinite and will eventually run out, at which time the landlord will be able to evict the occupier wholly legally, and without any need to give reasons, although he can normally only do this by issuing proceedings for possession in court. Eviction without a court order would normally be illegal: see Chapter 8.

Broadly, Tribunal jurisdiction is over a mixed bag of lettings which are still common forms of occupation in this country, but which the legislature has determined should not be accorded full protection. The largest class of such occupiers are tenants who have resident landlords; it also catches those who are provided with attendances or some, but not substantial, board; hostel-dwellers will frequently be within its jurisdiction, as will those in long-stay hotels. It does not cover, normally, lettings by landlords who are in some way publicly accountable (*e.g.* local authorities, housing associations) nor family/ friendly arrangements, nor those where no long-stay is involved.

In this Chapter, we shall consider:

1. *Lettings within Rent Tribunal jurisdiction*;
2. *Powers of the Tribunal as regards rent*;
3. *Powers of the Tribunal as regards security*; and
4. *Further Financial Protection*.

1. *Rent Tribunal Jurisdiction*

There are two ways that Tribunal jurisdiction is defined:

(i) Lettings brought within the jurisdiction by the general definition; and

(ii) Lettings brought within the jurisdiction by specific inclusion.

However, lettings can be excluded from the jurisdiction by:

(iii) Specific Exclusion.

(i) *General definition*

Tribunal jurisdiction is defined in section 19 of the Rent Act 1977. The Tribunal has jurisdiction over "contracts ... whereby one person grants to another person, in consideration of a rent which includes payment for the use of furniture or for services, the right to occupy a dwelling as a residence." In every case, it is the relationship between the occupier and the person who granted the right of occupation which is relevant: an occupier might be the restricted occupier of a protected tenant, or of an owner-occupier or, indeed, even of an unprotected tenant.

The use of the term "contracts" has been interpreted to include both tenancies and licences: *Luganda* v. *Service Hotels Ltd.* Services *includes* attendances (see Chapter 4, The Protected Tenant, (iv) p. 74)) and *also* the provision of heating or lighting, the supply of hot water and any other privilege or facility connected with the occupancy of a dwelling, other than a privilege or facility necessary for the purposes of access to the premises let, the supply of cold water or sanitary accommodation (section 85). None of these other services would qualify as an attendance within the definition at Chapter 1(iv). Furniture means any amount of furniture, not necessarily as much as would be needed to make the premises furnished in law under the pre-1974 legislation: see Chapter 4, 1(ii).

The arrangement has to be contractual, *i.e.* it has to be intended to be binding on the parties: see Chapter 2. It is also necessary to establish that rent is paid, for the Tribunal's jurisdiction is, first and foremost, one that regulates rents. This undoubtedly means money in normal circumstances, although, by analogy with the remarks made under 1(viii) in Chapter 4, a service tenant from whose wages a quantified amount was deducted at source would probably have no difficulty establishing that this constitutes payment of rent for these purposes (*Barnes* v. *Barratt*). Although in theory, the same remarks should be applicable to service occupiers, in practice this is so unlikely to be accepted by either Tribunal or a court that it would be wrong to extend the analogy. A service tenant will normally either be fully protected, or wholly unprotected. He is only likely to come within the Tribunal jurisdiction if he is living in the same building as his employer, but does not need to live there in order to do the job, or if an employer has provided an employee with accommodation in premises which he owns, as part of the contract of employment, but the accommodation happens to be in a house in which the tenants are provided with substantial attendance. Alternatively, it might be applicable if, under the terms of the contract, the employee was paying or having deducted from his wages such a low amount in respect of rent that the letting is excluded from full protection because the rent payable is less than two-thirds of the rateable value: see Chapter 4, The Protected Tenant, 1(iv), p.75, but does receive services or is provided with furniture.

Student lettings may be within Tribunal jurisdiction, even though they are excluded from full protection, provided that their lettings are furnished, or services are provided, as will commonly be the case. On the other hand, they may also be paying for board and this may be so substantial that they are excluded for this reason: see (iii), below.

The key element of Tribunal jurisdiction is that of exclusive occupation. A hostel-dweller who is given a room to share with another will not have exclusive occupation, unless the occupiers approached the hostel together and took the room as, as it were, joint licensees. Any tenant will have exclusive occupation: it has already been explained (at p. 38) that all tenants have exclusive possession, and that exclusive possession of definition includes exclusive occupation, while a licensee may have factual exclusive occupation not amounting to exclusive possession. In every case, it will be a question of fact whether or not an occupier has exclusive occupation. It will not be missing just because, for example, a landlord retains a key to the room, or because one of the landlord's employees comes in to clean.

(ii) *Specific inclusion*

Irrespective of whether a tenant would qualify under the general definition, above, the Rent Tribunal also has jurisdiction over the tenants of resident landlords who are excluded from full protection by reasons (i) and (ii) of Section 1, Chapter 4, and also those who are excluded from full protection under reason (iii), *i.e.* because they share living accommodation with their landlords. In any event, they will already have exclusive occupation, because they are tenants, and those excluded by reason (ii) will, of definition, be paying for furniture. Those excluded for reason (iv), provision of attendances to a substantial value-proportion of the rent, are included because they are paying for services, *i.e.* they are included under the general definition.

(iii) *Specific exclusion*

There are certain conditions which exclude an occupier from the jurisdiction of the Rent Tribunal, whether or not he qualifies under the general definition, or by specific inclusion:

(a) The rateable value of the (occupier's part of the) premises exceeds £1,500 (Greater London) or £750 (elsewhere). This is so unlikely to be the case that it may be assumed not to apply unless the landlord shows the contrary.

(b) The letting creates a regulated tenancy. This provision is inserted to ensure that there is no overlap between full protection and Rent Tribunal restriction.

(c) The landlord under the letting is the Crown or a government department. Local authorities are not expressly described as an exempt landlord but in practice other legislation effectively means that a tenant or licensee of the local authority will be unable to use the powers of the Rent Tribunal.

(d) The landlord under the tenancy is a Registered Housing Association, Housing Trust, the Housing Corporation or a housing co-operative. Note that this only excludes the *tenants* of such landlords, and does not preclude their licensees from using the powers of the Rent Tribunal, if they otherwise qualify.

(e) Under the terms of the letting, the occupier is provided with board and the value to the occupier of the board does not form a substantial proportion of the whole rent paid. This is a similar application of the test applicable to whether or not premises were let furnished in law before August 14, 1974, and whether or not sufficient attendances are provided to keep a tenancy out of protection (see Chap. 4, The Protected Tenant 1 (ii) and (iv) p. 72).) Board may be hard to value and is almost certainly worth more than the mere cost of the food. What constitutes board has been considered (at p. 75). If *any* board is provided, a tenancy cannot be protected; but if the value of the board forms an insubstantial proportion of the rent, then it will be restricted. Otherwise, it will be wholly outside of both protection and restriction.

(f) If the letting for the purposes of a holiday (see p. 76), the Rent Tribunal will not have jurisdiction over it.

2. *Rent Restriction*

In respect of all the lettings within its jurisdiction, the Rent Tribunal can fix a *reasonable* rent. That is to say, a rent which it considers reasonable in all the circumstances. There are no guidelines analogous to those to which the Rent Officer must pay heed, but, under different legislation, it has been decided that it would not be reasonable to make a tenant pay for general shortages in the availability of accommodation, *i.e.* scarcity value: *John Kay Ltd.* v. *Kay.*

In comparison to the systems of rent regulation considered in Chapter 4, Rent Tribunal powers over rents are very easy to describe indeed. An application may be made in respect of any letting within its jurisdiction, so long as the letting lasts, and the Tribunal can reduce, confirm or increase the existing rent. It can do this in respect of a periodic letting, or a fixed term letting, and irrespective of any contractually agreed rent. The Rent Tribunal rent, if one exists in respect of the letting, forms the only rent limit which binds the landlord.

Application forms are available from the Rent Tribunal office, or from a local aid or advice agency. A copy will be sent to the other side, *e.g.* a landlord on a tenant's application, who will have an opportunity to reply. If there are joint occupiers, of indeed joint landlords, then they must all sign the application, or else one must sign as agent for the others. The application can be made by landlord, or occupier, or both jointly, or by the local authority. As in most cases landlord and occupier will be living in the same premises, the local authority's power to refer rents should be used that much more frequently as a way of avoiding hostility between the parties.

Unlike an application to the Rent Officer which cannot normally be made until three years have passed since an earlier registration of rent, an application to the Rent Tribunal *can* be made at any time. However, the Tribunal is not obliged to hear an application made in less than three years unless there has been such a change in the condition of the dwelling, the furniture or services provided, the terms of the contract, or any other circumstances taken into account when the rent was last considered as to make the registered rent no longer reasonable. They must also hear an application in less than three years if the application is a joint application.

Like the Rent Officer, a Rent Tribunal registers a rent exclusive of rates, but will note that the actual rent payable is an inclusive rent, as will almost invariably be the case. If there is a fair rent registered for the premises, even though it is now let out on a tenancy which is not protected, then the Tribunal may not register a lower rent for the restricted letting than the fair rent on the register. In practice, Rent Tribunal rents are noticeably higher than fair rents, although it is very hard indeed to understand why this should be so, especially as the members selected to sit on the Rent Tribunal are drawn from exactly the same group of people who make up Rent Assessment Committees.

Once a rent is registered with the Rent Tribunal then that too, like the fair rent, normally remains effective indefinitely, or until a new application is made, even on a subsequent letting and even between wholly different parties. The one exception to this is that the Rent Tribunal has power to order that the registration shall in fact lapse after a particular period of time. This is rarely exercised but when it is, then the registration lapses after that and the position is subsequently as if there had never been any registration. Like the fair rent, too, the registered rent only bites on exactly the same premises, *i.e.* neither larger nor smaller.

If an occupier enters into a contract which is a restricted letting at a rent higher than a registered rent in force, then the excess rent paid is recoverable. This is recoverable for up to six years after it has been paid. There is, however, no provision for recovery of the overpaid rent by way of deduction from future rent and the occupier must, therefore, reclaim it as a civil debt, in the normal way: see Appendix 1. A major difference from the overcharging of a fair rent is that it is a criminal offence to overcharge a Rent Tribunal rent and this should be reported to the Tenancy Relations or Harassment Officer: see Chapter 8.

Rent Tribunals, like Rent Officers, are not obliged to visit premises in question, but will usually do so. They are, however, obliged to hold a hearing. In the normal course of events, the Tribunal members will visit the premises in the morning, and hold a hearing in the afternoon. The hearing will not be as formal as a court hearing, but will be more formal than that before the Rent Officer. The Tribunal will consist of three people, and the chairman will normally be a lawyer. Legal aid is not available for proceedings before a Rent Tribunal, but legal advice may be sought beforehand: see Appendix 2.

The Tribunal takes a fairly active part in the proceedings, asking questions and seeking out the information it is most interested in. It tends to disregard many of the frequently unfounded, gratuitous and commonly offensive allegations made of all manner of appalling behaviour by landlords who resent the official intervention in the rent he has agreed with the occupier. The occupier should try not to rise to this sort of bait and will usually need to do nothing more than deny the allegations, quietly and with dignity, indicating that he is happy to answer any questions about them that the Tribunal may wish to put to him. The Tribunal does not normally permit, and always discourages, cross-examination. If there is a dispute as to exactly what services or furniture are provided, it prefers to ask each party separately than to allow a face-to-face confrontation to develop, often into a brawl, in front of it. As when considering security, Tribunals usually take a fairly robust and realistic view of what is said before them. This is discussed further, under 3, below.

There is no provision for backdating rent to the date of application, nor need any notice of increase be served, nor do any phasing provisions apply. The essence of Tribunal procedure is speed, informality, inexpensive arbitration, etc. There is no reason why a social worker should not assist a client before the Tribunal but the presence of lawyers is not encouraged, save where a point as to jurisdiction is involved. Like the Rent Officer, a Tribunal has power to make its own decision as to jurisdiction, which may be appealed to the Divisional Court or, in theory, referred to the county court. For particular reasons, which relate to security, and are therefore discussed under that heading, 3, below, it will normally be necessary to refer a decision of the Tribunal to the Divisional Court rather than to the county court.

All applications must be made while the letting is still in existence, *i.e.* before any notice or fixed period expires. Of particular relevance here are the remarks made in Chapter 2 "Licence,", (p. 31) about the time of expiry of a notice bringing a licence to an end. Such a notice will expire after any contractually agreed time or form of notice, *or* a reasonable period of time, whichever is the *longer*. It follows that a shouted order to "get out at once," or by the next day, will not expire as a notice bringing the licence to an end until a reasonable time has elapsed. It can, therefore, still be referred to the Tribunal although, for example, the day has passed.

If a Tribunal wrongly refuses jurisdiction over a letting and the county court later decides that the letting is a restricted letting, then, provided the letting is still in existence, a new application can be made and, even though three years may not have elapsed, the Tribunal will certainly hear it anew and will accept the decision of the county court as binding upon it.

3. *Rent Tribunal Security of Tenure*

All applications to the Rent Tribunal have to be applications for consideration of rent, even if rent is not really the problem. Applications may also be for security of tenure, but the Tribunal has no powers at all unless the application is made also for rent registration. An occupier can only apply for security of tenure if a notice bringing the right of occupation to an end has been given — and not yet expired. This means that a fixed term agreement cannot be referred to the Tribunal for security of tenure. It can, however, before the time runs out, be referred for consideration of rent.

A restricted tenancy requires notice to quit in all its common law validity, in writing, of a minimum period of four weeks, and containing the prescribed information described in Chapter 2, "Tenancy," p. 35). Anything less will not be a valid notice to quit and the Tribunal neither can nor need bother to consider it. The tenancy continues as if nothing has happened. But no formalities other than those already referred to need to be fulfilled to bring a licence to an end.

Once a rent has been referred to the Tribunal, *i.e.* an application has been made, then any notice served before the application is automatically suspended and will not take effect until at least seven days after the hearing and the Tribunal decision, although customarily longer because of the security given by the Tribunal.

If a notice has been served before application, then the Tribunal will not only decide what rent is payable under the letting, but also when the notice should take effect. It can defer the notice for up to six months at a time. Before the six months runs out, there is nothing to stop an occupier applying for more time. In the pre-Rent Act 1974 days, when the majority of applications were by furnished tenants, the Rent Tribunals frequently granted two or more extensions of six

months. Now that most lettings which are referred to it will be
by the tenants of resident landlords, it may be less inclined to
grant security of as much as a year or more, by way of successive applications. The Tribunal may order no security at all, or
a period shorter than six months.

If no notice has been served by the time the application to
the Tribunal is made, then different provisions apply in the
event of a retaliatory notice following the application. These
apply whether notice is served between application and hearing, or after the hearing. Unless at the hearing for rent registration the Tribunal orders that a shorter period will be appropriate, any such notice will automatically be deferred, without
any need to re-apply to the Tribunal, for six months from the
date of the decision, *i.e.* usually, the date of the hearing.

The attitude of Tribunals to security will vary from Tribunal
to Tribunal. Some Tribunals take a very concerned line, especially where there is a resident landlord, and consider that the best
thing for all parties will be for them to be separated fairly soon.
Others, who will also give short periods of security, frankly dis-
agree with the idea that a landlord should not be able to decamp
an occupier from a house in which he is himself living. In either
case, the Tribunal should be reminded of the difficulties faced
by occupiers in finding somewhere else to live and reminded that
the *raison d'etre* of their security powers is this very problem.

Other Tribunals take a much more robust view, accepting
without qualm the theory that if a landlord wants to make
money out of a letting, then he must take the chance of having
in his home an occupier with whom he cannot get along. Most
Tribunals take a similarly robust view of what is said before it,
usually by a landlord declaring what a bad occupier the
individual in question is. The Tribunal will have had an
opportunity to see for itself just how well or otherwise an
occupier keeps premises and, indeed, in what state of repair
the landlord keeps the house.

There is in practice no appeal from a decision of the
Tribunal as to how much security to grant. Unless it can be
shown that it has taken account of some consideration it ought
to have excluded or, for example, offended the rules of natural
justice by refusing to hear an occupier's side of the story, no
higher court will interfere.

Problems arise when a Tribunal wrongly refuses to use its powers because it decides that it does not have jurisdiction over the letting. This is what happened in the case of *R. v. South Middlesex Rent Tribunal, ex parte Beswick*. Ms Beswick was the occupier of a single room in a YWCA hostel. Furniture and services were provided, and a weekly rent paid. Notice to leave was given and she referred this to the Rent Tribunal for the area. Unfortunately, on a misconstruction of the effect of the Rent Act 1974, the Tribunal wrongly decided that it did not have jurisdiction over the letting.

In theory, it should have been possible to go to the county court for a decision in point, in which case the Tribunal would no doubt have accepted its superior authority and heard the matter. However, by the time the case could have been heard in the county court, her notice would certainly have expired. The county court would have no power to reinstate it. The Tribunal would, therefore, have had no contract to consider, as it would have ended. This will happen in every case where the application to the Tribunal is in respect of a periodic letting, for cases do not come on before the county court within what will normally be only a four week period.

Instead, Ms Beswick had to take her case to the Divisional Court. For that court has power to quash the decision of the Rent Tribunal. By quashing the decision, the result is that in law no decision at all has been made and, therefore, the notice is still lodged with the Tribunal and automatically suspended pending a decision. In effect, their decision reactivated the notice, and the Tribunal jurisdiction. In practice, in every case where jurisdiction is in issue, the only course of action is to refer the matter to the Divisional Court.

Whether security has been gained because an application was made after a notice was served, or because the notice has followed rent registration and been automatically deferred, a landlord can reapply during the period for which the occupier has security of tenure for a reduction in that security. The Tribunal will grant a reduction of such period of time as it thinks fit, if it appears to the Tribunal that:

(a) the occupier has not complied with the terms of the contract;

(b) the occupier or anyone living with the occupier has been guilty of conduct which is a nuisance or annoyance to adjoining occupiers, which will commonly include the landlord as most cases now involve resident landlords, or has been convicted of using the premises or allowing them to be used, for an immoral or illegal purpose; or

(c) that the condition of the property or any furniture provided by the landlord has deteriorated because of the default of the occupier or anyone living with him.

If the Tribunal makes an order for reduced security, then no further application for security can be made to it.

No tenant can be evicted without a court order. In normal circumstances, court proceedings cannot be commenced until notice has expired (Chapter 2). However, where the letting is one which only continues in existence because of Tribunal security, then the landlord can commence proceedings even before that security runs out and the county court can make an order for possession, in effect reducing the Tribunal security, on — but only on — exactly the same grounds as those which will give the Tribunal power to reduce security. Like the Tribunal, it is not obliged to reduce security, and it can use the power by reducing security by such amount as it thinks fit.

In normal circumstances, a court making an order for possession against a restricted occupier will make what was described in Chapter Four (p. 82) as an outright order, that is to say one that will be suspended for 28 days. If the former restricted occupier was a licensee, then the landlord can use the speedy procedures, Orders 26 and 113, but this he cannot do in the case of a former restricted tenant.

None of the security provisions benefit an occupier on whom has been served, no later than at the beginning of the right of occupation, a notice in writing by the landlord that he has formerly occupied the premises himself *if*, at the time the notice to leave is to take effect, the landlord actually requires possession for use of the premises as a residence by himself or another member of his family who lived with him when last the landlord used the premises as his own residence. This provision does not apply to a landlord who is already living in another part of the same building. This makes use of the provisions somewhat infrequent now. It was originally designed to benefit people, *e.g.* going abroad for a time, who let out their property fully furnished while they were away. It could still apply if, for example, attendances were provided. There are analogous provisions for temporarily absent owner-occupiers where the tenancy is a protected tenancy, see Chapter 4, 2(iii).

4. *Further financial protection*

(i) *Premiums and deposits*

The prohibition against premiums and deposits described in Chapter 4, "Further Financial Protection" 4(i) p. 102), only apply to restricted lettings if there is an effective rent registration with the Rent Tribunal, *i.e.* one which applies to the letting in question. If there is not, then there are no prohibitions on deposits and premiums. But if a rent registered with the Tribunal does apply to the letting, then all the remarks made under this heading in Chapter 4 will apply in the same way.

(ii) *Accommodation agency charges* and

(iii) *Resale of utilities*

These both apply to restricted lettings in the same way that they apply to protected tenancies. See Chapter 4, 4(ii) and (iii).

6 No and Basic Security

In this Chapter, we shall examine the remaining forms of occupation:

1. *Trespassers*;
2. *Unrestricted Licensees*;
3. *Public Tenants*;
4. *Quasi-Public Tenants*; and
5. *Unrestricted Tenants*.

In addition, we shall consider (6) *Further Financial Protection* applicable to all but trespassers.

1. *Trespassers*

Trepassers have no rights of occupation and, because they pay no rent, are subject to no rent control. They have the least security of all. Court proceedings can be taken against them at any time, without any warning, and the speedy procedures referred to in Chapter 2 can, and in all probability will be used: Order 26 (county court) and Order 113 (High Court).

These procedures do not even require the landlord to identify the occupiers. A landlord can issue proceedings against a named person on his own, or against persons unknown, or against both a named person and persons unknown. A summons is issued, stating the landlord's interest in the property, that the property in question has been occupied without his consent and, if the summons is also against persons unknown, that the landlord does not know the names of some or all of the people on the property.

Once the summons is served, which can be by personal service but can also be, in the case of persons unknown, by fixing the summons to the door of the premises, there need only be a delay of five days before a court hearing. If the court finds that the occupiers are, indeed, trespassers, then it is obliged to make an immediate order for possession (*McPhail* v. *Persons Unknown*), not even subject to the normal 28 day delay which, for example, a final order against a protected or, indeed, any other tenant will normally be subject to. Landlords will still normally need to effect eviction by using court bailiffs, which may provide some slight delay of, perhaps, a week or 10 days: see Appendix 1. When bailiffs attend on an eviction, they must turn out of the premises all those people found there, whether or not they were parties to the proceedings, or even if they moved into the premises between court order and actual eviction, unless the occupier can maintain a claim to have some separate right of occupation, *e.g.* a tenant who is on the premises (*R.* v. *Wandsworth County Court, ex parte London Borough of Wandsworth*).

Although the court is obliged to make the immediate order, it is possible that the landlords will consent to a suspension of, for example, two or four weeks. This they may agree to before the actual hearing. If there is any prospect of a dispute, representatives of the landlord are likely to be amenable to granting such a delay in exchange for a decision by the occupier not to fight the case. Even if there is no prospect of a dispute, more responsible landlords, such as the public and quasi-public landlords the rights of whose tenants are described below, will usually be willing to agree to some time. If no agreement is reached between the parties before the hearing is called into court, it is still worthwhile asking the judge for a period of delay. The judge will state that he has no power to order such a delay but will invariably at the least ask the landlords' representative, and will often strongly urge him, to agree to a suspension. A lawyer who appears frequently in front of the same judge may be unwilling to disregard any such forceful request from the court.

Although the court can order costs against an occupier during the course of proceedings brought under one of these speedy procedures, there is no provision for awarding any monetary compensation by way of damages to the landlord. If a landlord wants to seek such damages, he must use normal possession proceedings and claim "mesne profits" in the way described in Appendix 1.

The only protection that a trespasser has against eviction is such as is provided by the Criminal Law Act 1977, which creates certain offences in connection with squatting, and also repeals the earlier Forcible Entry Acts. However, the Act also creates offences which a trespasser may commit in connection with squatting and it is far more likely that it is these latter offences which will see the light of court day than the former. Anyone who commits a criminal offence under the Criminal Law Act 1977 in the course of evicting a trespasser who is using premises as a residence is likely also to commit an offence under the Protection From Eviction Act 1977: see Chapter 8.

The offence which serves to protect trespassers is that of

(i) Violent eviction.

The offences a trespasser must be careful not to commit are those of:

(ii) Trespass with an offensive weapon;

(iii) Trespass on diplomatic or consular premises;

(iv) Resisting or obstructing an officer of a court in the course of an eviction;

(v) Refusing to leave premises when requested.

(i) *Violent eviction*

Any person, whether or not the landlord, who uses or threatens violence against either people or property in order to gain entry into premises, commits an offence if, but only if, the person seeking entry knows that there is someone present on the premises at the time of the attempted entry, and that that person is opposed to the entry. The offence is, of course, not committed if the person seeking entry has lawful authority to do so, *i.e.* a court bailiff. It does not constitute lawful authority that the person trying to get in has some greater interest, *e.g.* licence, tenancy or ownership of the property.

There is an important exception to this offence. The offence is not committed by a person otherwise offending against its provisions if he is a displaced residential occupier of the premises. A displaced residential occupier is any person, other than another trespasser, who was using the premises or part of them as a residence immediately before the trespasser entered. This exception is designed to permit the owner-occupier, or tenant, who goes away on holiday and finds on his return that the premises have been "squatted" to evict the trespassers without any need to take court proceedings and without fear of committing an offence. In practice, such incidents of squatting in people's homes have been almost unknown, as it is no part of the ethos of the squatter to make another homeless. A displaced residential occupier must also take great care using what some have described as a legislative incentive to violence for he may still commit any of the ordinary, criminal offences of assault, actual or grievous bodily harm, etc.

(ii) *Trespass with an offensive weapon*

It is a criminal offence for a person on premises as a trespasser, having entered as such, to have with him any weapon of offence, *i.e.* anything which has been made or adapted for causing injury to another. This, too, raises the spectre of "violent squatting' which has been virtually unknown in the recent history of the squatting movement. Because such a weapon can either be made or adapted for causing violence, a person can, in theory, be charged with it on the basis of possession of virtually any common household implement, *e.g.* a kitchen knife or a screwdriver.

The qualification is that the person committing the offence must not only be a trespasser, but must have entered as such. This refers to the common law rule that a former licensee and, strictly, even a former tenant, remaining on premises after the end of the licence or tenancy, becomes a trespasser: see Chapter 2. Such people are not trespassers for the purposes of this provision.

(iii) *Trespass on diplomatic or consuler premises*

This provision was designed to deal with "political squatting" (*Kamara* v. *DPP*) and makes it an offence for a trespasser to enter diplomatic or consuler buildings, unless he can show that he did not believe them to be diplomatic or consular premises.

(iv) *Resisting or obstructing an officer of the court in the course of an eviction*

It is an offence to resist or *intentionally* obstruct any person who is in fact an officer of a court executing a possession order issued by a county court or the High Court. This offence is only committed by someone in premises in circumstances that are also defined in the Act. Shortly, the Act is intended to catch anyone resisting or intentionally obstructing an officer who is executing a possession order made under one of the speedy procedures described above, Orders 26 and 113. However, it is so worded that it applies to resistance or intentional obstruction of an officer executing any order which *could* have been brought under those procedures, *i.e.* if the landlord chooses to use normal proceedings, instead of the special, speedy procedures, for example because he wishes to claim damages for use and occupation. The Orders can be used against any trespasser, which includes former licensees and has also been held to include illegal subtenants (*Moore Properties (Ilford) Ltd.* v. *McKeon*): see Chapter 2. The Orders do *not* catch illegal tenants of mortgagors (*London Goldhawk Buildings Society* v. *Eminer and another*): see Chapter 2.

(v) *Refusing to leave premises when requested*

This is the major new offence introduced by the Act (section 7). It makes it an offence for any trespasser, who entered as a trespasser, to fail to leave premises if asked to do so by a displaced residential occupier or by a person who is, within the terms of the Act, a protected intending occupier. Displaced residential occupier has been described under (i), above.

The provisions relating to protected intending occupiers have been designed to deal with another situation which squatters were often accused of creating but that was, in fact, also comparatively rare. That is to say, that squatters were occupying premises intended for the occupation of someone else, *e.g.* a person on the housing waiting list. The definition of displaced residential occupier in the Act includes more would-be occupiers than these alone; it includes those who buy residential property only to find that it has been occupied during the period it lay vacant while the sale was being transacted.

A person is a protected intending occupier if he either has a freehold or a leasehold interest in the property, and requires the premises for his own occupation. The leasehold interest has to actually have not less than 21 years to run at the relevant time. A person is also a protected intending occupier if he has been given permission to occupy the premises as a residence by any of the public or quasi-public landlords described below. In either case, the protected intending occupier must be kept out of occupation by reason of the trespass and, obviously, there can be no offence of failing to leave when requested, until a request has been made.

The request does not need itself to be in writing but protected intending occupiers need to produce statements which prove the status of protected intending occupier. In the first case, the statement has to specify the interest which the would-be occupier has, to state the requirement for use of the premises as a residence for himself, and must have been signed either in the presence of a justice of the peace or commissioner of oaths who has also signed the statement as a witness. In the second case, the statement must specify that the would-be occupier has been authorised to occupy the premises and that the landlord is one of the bodies referred to.

It is clear that a protected intending occupier could be a licensee, *e.g.* for short-life use, of one of the public or quasi-public landlords; and it is also clear that as it is necessary for a protected intending occupier to specify that the premises are to be used as a residence, it can only be used in connection with premises fit for such use, *i.e.* not in connection with premises yet to be renewed or redeveloped. It is a defence for the trespasser to prove that he did not believe that the person asking him to leave was either a displaced residential occupier or a protected intending occupier, or that the premises in question are or form part of premises used mainly for non-residential purpose and that he was only on that part. It is also a defence to prove that a protected intending occupier did not produce a statement like those described in the last paragraph.

Eviction of trespassers often happens in highly-charged circumstances. It can be extremely distressing for the occupier who, after all, if he had any other accommodation available, would not have been putting up with the attendant insecurity of trespass in the first place. A social worker involved in such a situation will have much to offer if he can ensure that no offences are committed by the trespasser, and can also ensure that the correct procedure is used by the person attempting to evict the trespasser for, save in the circumstances described, the broad and general intention of the law is that people should not, where practicable, be evicted from premises they are using as a home without the time to make alternative arrangements produced by due legal proceedings.

2. *Unrestricted Licensees*

There are two sorts of licensee who will not enjoy any statutory protection at all and who must therefore rely upon their common law rights of occupation. The first is the bare licensee, *i.e.* members of family, friends and other informal arrangements not intended by the parties to be contractually binding, and contractual licensees whose contracts do not come within the jurisdiction of the Rent Tribunal, for example because too much board is provided, or because no money is paid, or because the property is a short-life property, and as such a licence, but the rent does not include payment for furniture or service. Service occupiers will also normally be unrestricted licensees.

At common law, no licensee can be evicted until the licence has been brought to an end. A bare licence can be brought to an end by reasonable notice, and a contractual licence by either reasonable notice or the contractually agreed period (and form), whichever is the longer. A fixed term contractual licensee requires no notice and the licence terminates on the expiry of the term. An example of such an arrangement might be a letting for short-life use which is for a specific period only.

There is no rent control for the contractual licensee who does not fall within Rent Tribunal jurisdiction. Strictly, such an occupier's rent cannot be increased without terminating the existing licence, in the normal way, and offering a new one. However, most licensees simply consent to a mutual variation of the terms as regards the rent unless they are actually prepared to leave for, lacking any legislative protection, they are in no bargaining position at all.

Once the licence has terminated, the former licensee is in strict law a trespasser. Indeed, both the former bare licensee and the former contractual licensee are in exactly the same position as a trespasser (see 1. above), save that they are not liable to be convicted for certain of the offences described. A service occupier is, however, in a different position as regards eviction.

All former licensees, including service occupiers, are within the scope of the speedy procedures, Orders 26 and 113. It is always necessary to take legal proceedings to evict a former service occupier, who enjoys a special privilege of remaining in occupation until a court order is made, provided that he enjoyed exclusive occupation of the premises which he held with his job: Protection From Eviction Act 1977 ss. 3 and 8. In all other cases, it is practicable and advisable to take court proceedings to evict a former licensee, because there is a risk that if a landlord does not do so, he will commit a criminal offence, for example under the Criminal Law Act 1977, or common law assault, etc. If a landlord commits a criminal offence in evicting a former licensee, then he will also commit an offence under the Protection From Eviction Act 1977, see Chapter 8.

The offence which a landlord is most likely to commit is that of violent eviction, described at 1(i), above. A landlord could not defend such a charge on the ground that he is a displaced residential occupier. The definition of displaced residential occupier precludes this possibility. For a person to be a displaced residential occupier, he must show that he was occupying the premises as a resident *immediately* before the trespass. This, in the case of a former licensee, he could not do, for immediately before the trespass, the trespasser was occupying the premises as a resident not, of course, as a trespasser, but as a licensee.

Former licensees are not subject to proceedings for being on premises with an offensive weapon, nor are they required by law to leave when asked to go by a displaced residential occupier or a protected intending occupier. They can, however, commit the offence of resisting or intentionally obstructing an officer of the court in the execution of an order of the court for possession, because they are all liable to Orders

26 and 113, even if those proceedings are not actually used against them, for example, because the landlord was claiming damages for use and occupation during or continuing after the licence and therefore chose to use normal possession proceedings: see Appendix 1.

The protection which has been described is paltry indeed. There is a widespread popular belief that no one can be evicted from his home without a court order. Those who had not appreciated the lack of security that they have enjoyed, will often find it both curious and dismaying that they can be so summarily evicted. At the same time, it will only be a greater distress to them if they continue to hold out false expectations, possibly leading to the defence of court proceedings which are, in short, indefensible and even, in some circumstances, perhaps running up liability to legal costs. On the other hand, the proposition stated in the last paragraph of 1, above, that the law intends that most occupiers should only be evicted through court proceedings is one that ought to encourage landlords to use the court before regaining possession.

3. *Public Tenants*

Those who are described as public tenants are the tenants of the Crown, a government department or a local authority. The position as regards the latter is slightly different than that which applies to either of the former. However, *all* former tenants are entitled to remain in occupation until such time as a court order is obtained against them, Protection From Eviction Act 1977, s. 3, and it would be illegal eviction to regain possession in any other way: see Chapter 8.

It is, of course, equally illegal to evict a tenant before the expiry of the tenancy. The rules relating to determination or expiry of a tenancy have been dealt with in Chapter 2. None of the requirements for the provision of information which apply to protected and restricted tenants apply to any of the tenancies under discussion in this Chapter. However, notices to quit must still be in writing and must of of a minimum period of four weeks and are subject to the other common law rules described in Chapter 2, "Tenancy," p. 32.

There is no rent control of the public tenant. Normally, in order to increase the rent, the landlord must bring the tenancy to an end in the usual way and, of course, in the case of a fixed term tenancy, he will not be able to do that simply in order to raise the rent. A fixed term tenant could consent to an increase during the period, but it is fairly likely to be unenforceable should he subsequently change his mind, because, in effect, the landlord will have given nothing in exchange for the increase. A periodic tenant could likewise consent to the increase without compelling the landlord to serve notice to quit and offer a new tenancy, but this might be enforceable because of the ease with which the landlord could otherwise bring the tenancy to an end. It is for this reason that many public periodic tenants would be inclined to consent to an increase. It should be said that the public landlords, under discussion here, are normally quite reasonable about· rents and they are, of course, subject to both political and public pressures in a way that usually does not touch the private landlord.

Local authorities are under an obligation to keep rents in their areas under review; however, they also have a discretion to charge such rents as they consider reasonable. This has nothing to do with the reasonable rent charged by the Rent Tribunal. Local authority tenancies are almost invariably periodic. They have a particular privilege, contained in section 12 of the Prices and Incomes Act 1968, to raise rents without serving a notice to quit. They may, instead, serve a notice of increase. This cannot take effect earlier than the authority could otherwise have brought the tenancy to an end by notice to quit, *i.e.* not less than four weeks, and the notice must warn the tenant of his right to leave rather than pay the increase. In addition, the notice must tell the tenant what he must do to bring the tenancy to an end if he chooses to leave, and by what date the tenant must serve his own notice to quit to the local authority, if that is what he is choosing to do.

Local authority rents are traditionally lower than those registered by the Rent Officer. From 1972-73, there was a move to raise them all to the same level, but these provisions were repealed by the Housing Rents and Subsidies Act 1975. The spirit and intention of public housing is, of course, one that recognises the obligation of society as a whole to provide decent housing for all. Traditionally, local authority housing has been used to provide for the working class and over this century there has been a gradual shift of more than half the tenanted occupation out of the private sector into the public. One argument in favour of the lower rents enjoyed by local authority tenants is their lack of security: however, this is likely soon to be altered. The principal determining factor is that local authority housing is not and should not be run as a business enterprise. Nonetheless, local authority rents have gradually been catching up with fair rents and it is likely that in the not too distant future, there will be little difference between them. Indeed, there has always been some political pressure on government to ensure that local authority tenants do not pay markedly less than private tenants and some see recent suggestions that the fair rent system may be amended to allow higher rents (see Chapter 1) as a prelude to an increase of rents in the public sector also.

As regards security, although local authority tenants enjoy no security of tenure as such, authorities are obliged by common law to act within their powers. Powers are so defined at law as to preclude authorities acting in an unreasonable fashion, and to require authorities to act reasonably. Where eviction is concerned, this means that a local authority could not serve a notice to quit, *e.g.* whimsically. Before making a decision to evict, the authority must take into account all proper and reasonable considerations, and must exclude from consideration anything which it would be improper to take into account. For example, a corrupt decision will always be outside its powers, as will a decision borne of malice.

It is more likely that the authority will have failed to take into account relevant considerations. These include such directions or guidance as the authority may have been given by the Department of the Environment. In Ministerial Circulars 74/72 and 18/74, local authorities were urged to consider, before deciding to evict a tenant, the question of the home-lessness that might follow (see Chapter 10), social services legis-lation, rent and rate rebates (see Chapter 7), the possibility of suing a tenant in arrears simply for the civil debt, not for both possession and arrears at the same time, attachment of earnings order, social work assistance, etc.

The underlying theme is that local authorities ought to try other solutions to, in particular, rent arrears and not simply decide to evict. Previous practice — which by and large continues unabated — was for the local authority with a tenant in arrears to serve notice to quit and seek a possession order and judgement for the arrears. In practice, if the tenant made an offer to clear the arrears within a reasonable time, the notice would not be withdrawn, nor the summons, but the authority would consent to the court making an order for possession suspended so long as the current rent plus a stated figure off the arrears each week was paid. The court would have no such power without consent as it does not enjoy the Rent Act powers of suspension where the Rent Act does not apply. This is a heavy-handed approach, indeed, and leaves an intimidating weapon hanging over the head of the tenant.

In the case of *Bristol District Council* v. *Clark*, the Court of Appeal held that an authority which completely disregarded those ministerial circulars would be acting improperly and that, in consequence, a court would not enforce its notice to quit or summons for possession. But complete disregard is something very different from choosing not to follow the guidance in the circulars and it will be a sufficient defence for an authority to show that they had in mind the possibilities discussed in those circulars, but elected not to apply them, or, if you like, decided they were inappropriate. Furthermore, in *Cannock Chase District Council* v. *Kelly*, it was held that there was no obligation on a local authority to state its reasons for an eviction so that even a tenant with no record of misbehaviour could be evicted. Unless he was in a position to point to some improper consideration by the local authority, or some failure of the local authority to have regard to the circulars or any other relevant matter, the decision to evict could not be defended.

A social worker will normally be in an excellent position to use his status on a local authority employee to put pressure on a housing authority — which may not be the same authority — not to evict where appropriate, or to discuss with the housing authority the most appropriate steps to take. In particular, both social worker and housing authority should have in mind the provisions of the Housing (Homeless Persons) Act 1977; see Chapter 10.

4. *Quasi-Public Tenants*

These are the tenants of Registered Housing Associations, Housing Trusts, the Housing Corporation and housing co-operatives. Housing Trusts have been in existence for some time, but Housing Associations are a comparatively recent development. Both seek to do no more than provide housing, either for specified classes of people or else more generally for those in need of housing, and are neither intended nor permitted to make any profit out of their operations. There are, of course, no shareholders and such surplus as is produced must, legally, be ploughed back into further housing operations. Both can and do receive state subsidies for their operations, although it is the housing associations which receive the most and which constitute the largest quasi-public sector of housing operations.

In addition, the Housing Corporation, which is the central body governing the quasi-public sector, is empowered to manage property and any tenancies they grant are outside of protection. The most recent development in the quasi-public sector is that of housing co-operatives. They may shortly be described as bodies in which the occupiers of the housing together constitute the management body itself. They are subject to the government of the Housing Corporation, and also receive extensive state subsidies for purchase of housing and, in the early days, renovation and repair of premises, and must also plough any profits from rent back into housing operations.

All of these bodies charge fair rents. There are separate parts of the rent register kept for such registrations. In most respects, the procedure is the same as that for protected tenancies; see Chapter 4, Protection of Rents, 3, on p. 88). There are two principal distinctions: first of all, there is a right for the landlord to appeal to the Secretary of State for the Environment to increase a fair rent beyond that assessed, finally, by the Rent Assessment Committee, on the grounds that it cannot otherwise sustain its operations. It is extremely likely that this power will be used, if at all, very sparingly.

The second distinction is that the quasi-public landlords enjoy a similar privilege to increase rents under periodic tenancies without serving notice to quit, by serving a notice of increase like that which local authorities can use (see 3, above), *i.e.* it cannot take effect before a notice to quit could have done so.

There is no analogous requirement on a quasi-public landlord to act reasonably, but any eviction in contravention of the constitution of the landlord body would also be illegal and unenforceable in law.

5. *Unrestricted Tenants*

This class will include the tenant who is provided with substantial board and the tenant occupying premises of very high rateable value. There are few of either sort of tenancy in existence, especially since many if not most of those receiving board will be considered licensees rather than tenants, following the decision in *Marchant* v. *Charters* (Chapter 2). Unrestricted tenants enjoy the protection of their contracts against both eviction and rent increase but are in a weak bargaining position when it comes to increases as the landlord can easily terminate the tenancy, *e.g.* if it is a periodic tenancy. The notice to quit must be in writing, and of a minimum of four weeks, and must otherwise comply with the common law, but need not contain the prescribed information.

All tenants can only be evicted by due process of law and they cannot be proceeded against under Orders 26 and 113. Normal county court proceedings for possession are considered in Appendix 1.

6. *Further Additional Financial Protection*

As trespassers do not pay for their occupation of premises, there is no financial protection available to them. However, all of the other classes described in this chapter are subject to protection in respect of

(i) Accommodation agency charges; and

(ii) Resale of utilities.

There are no restrictions on the charging of premiums which apply to these classes of occupation.

Both the restrictions on accommodation agency charges and those on the resale of utilities apply to the classes of occupation described in this Chapter as they do to restricted and protected tenants. See Chapter 4, Further Financial Protection (ii) and (iii) p. 104.

7 Financial Assistance

All of the law studied in this book up to this point has dealt with regulation of the relationship between landlord and tenant, principally as regards rights of occupation and rents. The matters under consideration in this chapter are of a different quality, for they affect the rights of individual occupiers in relation to the state. The topics to be considered in this Chapter are:
1. *Welfare Benefits*; and
2. *Relocation Allowances*.

1. *Welfare Benefits*

It is not proposed to consider here the full range of welfare benefits available to any individual. There are, of course, other books which undertake that task, and easily the most readable and, for a social worker, an indispensible guide is the annual *National Welfare Benefits Handbook*, edited by Ruth Lister and published by the Child Poverty Action Group (see Appendix 2.) We are concerned only with those benefits which relate directly to the housing situation. It is to some extent an artificial approach, because the majority of those in receipt of welfare benefits generally do not allocate one sum, for example, a rent allowance, to the rent, and Family Income Supplement to child maintenance but, rather, pool the whole of what will too often be an inadequate income and apply it as and how they can best do so.

The major problem with all welfare benefits is that of non-take-up. There are even people who have no income at all who do not appreciate their entitlement to receive, for example, supplementary benefit. The problem is most acute in relation to those benefits which people who are in employment and, therefore, in receipt of some income, are entitled to, for example, rent and rates rebates and rent allowance.

This is partly a problem of ignorance. If people are earning, and, especially if they are paying tax because their earnings do not fall below the tax threshholds, they do not realise that there may be other ways of recouping some at least of their money. A second, and not insignificant, contributor to the problem of non-take-up of benefit is the mass of bureaucracy which surrounds administration of the welfare benefits system. Different allowances are obtained from different offices and departments: *e.g.* Supplementary Benefit (SB) is administered by local offices of the Department of Health and Social Security (DHSS) but is governed centrally by the Supplementary Benefits Commission (SBC), while rebates and allowances for housing are granted by the local authority. Particularly where SB is concerned, claimants are subjected to massive queues in the offices, delays in consideration of their applications, delays in receipt of their entitlements, etc. It will not be uncommon to find that people who have once claimed, or attempted to do so, are reluctant, even under severe financial strictures, to put themselves through the official mill once again.

There is a third contributory factor to non-take-up of benefit and this too is an important influence. There is an inculcated reluctance amongst many people to ask for or receive what they may term "welfare" or, indeed, what they will often consider charity. A social worker will have to undertake on many occasions the task of explaining to people that there is no need for them to suffer from such an attitude. The welfare system in this country is, in effect, an integral part of the taxation programme: the state takes with one hand, and sometimes gives some back with the other. Both taxation and levels of rent, whether in the public or private sector, are calculated on an assumption that those who qualify can reclaim the due excess. It cannot be said that it is calculated on an assumption that they will do so, for experience of the benefits system suggests that it is frequently politically desirable to indicate that vast sums of money have been allocated to this benefit or to that, while safe in the knowledge that anything up to half of it will never actually be claimed.

(i) *Rent rebates*

Rent rebates are only available to the tenants of local authorities. The amount of rent rebate is calculated according to a number of variables:

(a) A needs allowance, which is usually changed from year to year, based on an individual's circumstances, including the size of family;

(b) The total income of the tenant and his spouse;

(c) The amount of rent being paid.

If there are joint tenants, the local authority will normally select one of them, the higher earner, and treat him as if he were the sole tenant, paying the rebate to him. Savings are ignored in calculation of entitlement, up to a specified amount. In 1976 this was £1200. It would not be worthwhile to reproduce here the current rates of entitlement as these are likely to be out-of-date by the time this book is read. Nor, given the number of variables, would it be a justifiable use of space to reproduce all the relevant tables.

The whole of the rent rebate and allowance scheme, which includes rent allowances and rates rebates, is subject to a power invested in local authorities, who administer the scheme, to increase national norms of entitlement by up to 10 per cent. This is in order to allow the local authority to take account of special factors affecting its own locality: a social worker may be in a good position to provide information to and pressure upon the authority to use this power.

Rent rebates must be claimed. They will not be automatically provided by the authority. Whether or not a person has been advised of his entitlement to rent rebate is one of the factors which a local authority ought to contemplate before making a decision to commence proceedings for possession of premises because of arrears of rent; see Chapter 6.

(ii) *Rent allowances*

This is the parallel scheme for tenants in the private sector. The levels of take-up of rent allowance are even lower than those which mark the rent rebate system. It does not matter what sort of private tenancy a person has, *e.g.* protected, restricted, quasi-public, unrestricted. If, however, under the terms of the tenancy any board or furniture is provided, the value of this will be assessed and deducted from the amount treated as rent payable for the purposes of calculation of allowance due.

The amount available under this system is calculated in the same way as is the rent rebate, *i.e.* on the basis of the same three factors. However, local authorities, in their role of administrators of the allowance, will not accept liability in full towards a rent which they consider excessive. If a rent has not been registered with the Rent Officer, they are more likely to treat as the rent payable that which they think the Rent Officer would register. This provides a fairly powerful incentive to the tenant to apply for registration. It is in exactly such circumstances that, if the tenant is at all reluctant to apply in his own name, the local authority should be urged to use its powers to refer the rent to the Rent Officer itself; see Chapter 4.

One difficulty this poses is that many tenants cannot apply to the Rent Officer at all. Rent Tribunal rents are customarily higher than those the Rent Officer registers: see Chapter 5. This puts the tenant in an intolerable position: unable to register for a lower rent, and unable to claim benefit for the full amount he is obliged to pay. There is no solution to this problem, other than a change of policy by an authority which applies such a 'criterion, and the Department of the Environment, which has central responsibility for the scheme, has not taken any opportunity to use its powers to avert this unequal result, despite being asked to do so.

A subtenant, who is genuinely a subtenant and not a sharer or lodger, *i.e.* licensee, is entitled to a rent allowance, but if the tenant is himself receiving either rent allowance or rent rebate, the amount of rent that the tenant is treated as paying, for the purpose of calculating his entitlement, will be reduced by the amount of rent received from the subtenant. A lodger or sharer cannot claim rent rebate or allowance or, indeed, as he will not be liable for the rates, a rates rebate.

As well as the power to make an "across the board" 10 per cent increase, a local authority can also grant rent rebates or allowances in excess of the local norm if "personal or domestic circumstances are exceptional." Wherever exceptional hardship is caused, it is worth asking the authority to exercise this power and a social worker may be able to help in such an application.

All application forms, whether for rent rebate or allowance, or for rates rebate, are available from the local housing department, or from the treasurer's department of the local authority, and also from most advice and aid agencies. It is possible to make representations to the local authority about a refusal of rebate or allowance, or about an award which is considered too low, but there is no independent or formal appeal system.

(iii) *Rates rebates*

These are available to any tenant, or houseowner, who is paying rates. It applies to both private and local authority tenants, and all other classes. It is available even to those who do not pay their rates directly, but who pay a rent inclusive of rates to the landlord. Rates rebates are also calculated on the basis of the same three variables referred to under (i) above, save that, of course, it is the amount of rates paid rather than rent which is relevant. There are two distinctions from the rent systems considered above; first of all, the local authority has no power to make an increase over the local norm in cases of individual exceptional hardship; and, secondly, different results will emerge in the event of a breakup of a relationship.

If a non-tenant spouse remains in occupation of the matrimonial home, a rent rebate or allowance will be available, even though the occupier is not strictly the tenant. But a rates rebate will not be available, because it is the departed tenant-spouse (or, in the case of owner-occupied property, the departed owner-spouse) who remains liable for the rates. The departed spouse may himself be able to claim a rate rebate, even though he is no longer living in the premises. And once a spouse succeeds in having either owner-occupied property or property subject to a protected tenancy transferred into his name (see Chapter 9), then he will qualify for rebate again. Rates rebates do not extend to water and sewage rates, *i.e.* they only apply to general rates.

There is, however, a wholly independent power, unrelated

to the rebate/allowance scheme, to reduce or refund rates payments "on account of the poverty of any person liable to pay." This power, which is invested in the local authority, is contained in section 53 of the General Rate Act 1967.

(iv) *Supplementary benefit*

People receive SB either because they have no income at all, or because their other income is below what is considered to be the basic subsistence level at which an individual, given his commitments, is expected to live. It is not available to those in full-time employment. People in receipt of unemployment or other social security benefits may have their allowances "topped up" by SB.

Those in receipt of SB do not qualify for rent or rates rebate or allowance. This is because their entitlement to SB is calculated so as to provide them with a "rent element." There are some transitional provisions for those already in receipt of rebate or allowance who go on to SB during a period for which they have already been given an award. As SB will take such receipts into account, there is no benefit to the claimant.

Those receiving SB should receive the full amount of rent and rates with their weekly allowance. However, the SB will only pay what they consider to be, for their purposes, a reasonable rent. This is not the same as a Rent Tribunal reasonable rent. It is, usually, a rent based on local knowledge and there is often, contrary to the policy of the SBC, an unofficial local "ceiling" beyond which officials will not pay. This produces particular hardship for those who do not pay local authority rents and cannot obtain registration of fair rents. In the main, rents at those levels will normally be met. Rents subject only to the jurisdiction of the Rent Tribunal will normally be much higher than the local ceiling, and so may be the rent of a wholly unrestricted tenant.

The SBC should be urged to compare what they are allowing by way of "rent element" to what the tenant is actually being required to pay. They do have the power to pay the full rent, and if it is clear that as a result of their refusal to pay the higher sum the occupier may lose his home, they may eventually be persuaded to do so. As most applications for registration of Rent Tribunal rents eventually result in eviction (see Chapter 5), the SBC should be dissuaded from compelling the tenant to apply to the Tribunal simply to fix a lower rent.

A full rent may also be refused because the SBC considers that the accommodation occupied is unreasonable for the person in question, for example, because it is unduly large or in an expensive area. The SBC can only reduce the rent element for this reason if the local authority for the area in question is prepared formally to endorse the view that the property is too big or in too luxurious an area for the claimant.

Those who are not actually tenants may encounter problems securing the full amount of the money they pay in rent. The provisions applicable to them are extremely complicated, especially when set against a study of housing law, for the SBC works out what is payable not by reference to known concepts of housing law but by reference to various different sorts of situation. Hostel-dwellers and those living in long-stay hotels, for example, will not receive any rent element at all, although their SB entitlement will be calculated so as to provide them with a fixed amount for lodging and board or, if no board is provided, for eating out, in addition to their normal personal expenses allowance.

Those who are living with family or friends are treated as "non-householders," and they will be given a fixed rent element which may, however, at the discretion of the office, be increased to the actual amount which they are paying by way of contribution to the householder. The officials will customarily treat other sharers, *e.g.* flatsharers, as non-householders, but it may be possible to argue against this. The basis of this argument is that there is no substantive or practical distinction between a flatsharer and a joint tenant and they should not, therefore, receive a less than full allowance. If this argument is successful, then sharers too may receive the full amount that they pay by way of rent.

Any amount received by a tenant who is himself claiming SB will be deducted from the estimate of his rent for the purposes of calculating his rent element. However, before this deduction is made, any actual expenses incurred from the subletting will be deducted, *e.g.* the cost of providing heating to a subtenant whose rent includes payment for heating. The same

will happen even when the other occupier is not on SB.
In normal circumstances, mortgagors on SB will only receive
the interest element of their monthly payments to the mortgage company. In addition, they will also receive any rates
paid, any ground rent payable, and a discretionary amount for
repairs and insurance. The interest payment will only be
allowed up to a reasonable amount, in relation to the size of
the property, area, needs, etc., or to an amount determined in
accordance with the test of whether the mortgage itself was a
reasonable expenditure at the time the mortgage was taken on,
i.e. given the individual occupier's resources at that time.

In addition to these benefits, there is always the possibility,
but usually only a slim possibility, of persuading the officials to
grant an Exceptional Needs Payment (ENP) or an Exceptional
Circumstances Addition (ECA) to a claimant in receipt of SB.
An ENP is a once-off payment which means exactly what it
says: something which the SBC has authority to pay in
exceptional need. In theory, a mortgagor who has to do major
repairs, more than can be paid for out of the repairs element
of the weekly allowance, could ask for an ENP with which to
pay for the work necessary. In practice, the SBC will be
reluctant to use this power and will instead urge the mortgagor
to take on a second mortgage, or get a loan from the local
authority under the powers described in the book *Housing:
Repairs and Improvements*. The amount of any extra interest
will, however, be added to the rent element of the claimant's
SB entitlement. An ENP might also be applied for by a
mortgagor threatened with eviction because of arrears of
repayments and, again in theory, the SBC has power to make
such a payment even although the arrears include a capital
element. In practice, it will be very hard indeed to get such a
payment from them. Exactly the same remarks apply to
arrears of rent.

An ECA is a regular payment of an additional sum which
recognises some regular, extra outgoing, *e.g.* a child who
requires special food for medical reasons. All SB payments are
subject to a right of appeal to an independent tribunal, the
Supplementary Benefit Appeal Tribunal. The rates of SB are
published, like those of the other benefits referred to in this
Chapter, in various leaflets, by local authorities and central

government departments, from time to time, as levels of
benefit and qualification change.

2. *Relocation Allowances*

In the earlier Chapters of this book, there has been reference
to the possibilities of compulsory relocation: both owner-
occupiers and other residents can be forced to move if a local
authority compulsorily purchases a property, under any of its
development powers although, most commonly, this will
happen as part of a policy of clearance of a particular area. In
addition, individual properties may become so run-down that
the authority puts a closing order or a demolition order on the
property, both of which have the effect of prohibiting further
occupation of it. As relocation normally occurs in the context
of disrepair, the subject of relocation allowances will be dealt
with in the book *Housing: Repairs and Improvements* in somewhat greater detail. The purpose of referring to them at all
here is to indicate to the reader what is available.

(i) *Compulsory purchase*

When property is compulsorily purchased, a local authority
has to pay for what it takes over. The amount paid will be as
calculated by the District Surveyor and may be based on
market value. Under certain circumstances, an owner-
occupier can serve notice on a local authority requiring it to
buy his house, for example, if a compulsory improvement
notice has been served in a Housing Action Area, or if a
demolition order is made by a local authority. In such cases,
something less than market value may be payable, and it may
be as little as mere site value. However, the "owner-occupier's
subsidy" may apply in such circumstances in order to put a
displaced owner-occupier in a position to buy a new house, or
at least not to find himself, for example, left with a mortgage
for much more than the site value he has received, on a
property which no longer exists. The purpose of this legislation
is to prevent private landlords actually making a gain out of
the public purse by allowing their properties to fall into such
disrepair that the authority either has to or can be forced to

purchase at a full market value, and their tenants wholly legally evicted: see Chapter 4, 2(ii).

(ii) *Home loss payment*

Anyone who has lived in property for five years is entitled to a home loss payment when he is compulsorily relocated, for example, because the local authority has purchased the property from his landlord and intends to clear or renovate it, or because a closing order has been placed on the property because it is unfit for occupation. The claim must be made, from the local authority, within 6 months of moving and the amount payable is 3 times the rateable value of the property, from a minimum payment of £150 to a maximum of £1500. This may also be available to a local authority tenant who is relocated because the property is no longer fit for human habitation, even although no formal closing order is made. When a closing or demolition order is made, or an occupier displaced as a result of compulsory purchase, the local authority is under a duty to rehouse if no alternative accommodation is available to the individual in question.

(iii) *Disturbance payment*

This is a sum available to one who does not qualify for home loss because he has not been living in the premises long enough. It is intended to provide for actual expenses incurred during removal, such as disconnection and reconnection of utilities, cost of redirecting mail, cost of adapting carpets or lino, etc. It may also be awarded for the cost of replacing furniture which will not fit into the new home. It is available as an additional amount to those who qualify for home loss.

8 Harassment and Illegal Eviction

One of the most common problems that a social worker will encounter in relation to housing is that of harassment and illegal eviction. It would be at the least disingenuous not to expect resentment from many landlords towards occupiers who are allowed to remain in occupation beyond their wishes and to pay rents below that which they consider appropriate. Landlords have, after all, a long history of absolute rights of proprietorship to encourage this attitude.

In Chapter 1, we considered some of the wiles adopted by landlords who seek to evade the effect of the Rent Act. But such comparatively sophisticated devices are not used by all. Many landlords, even in this day and age, still resort to brute force and other forms of cunning in order to get rid of their occupiers when they want. In the early 1960s, these tactics grew to such a pitch that legislation had to be introduced to cope with what came to be known by the name of the most famous exponent, Rachmanism. The legislation was contained in the Rent Act 1965 and has recently been consolidated into the Protection From Eviction Act 1977. It defines criminal offences of harassment and illegal eviction.

Regrettably, this legislation has not succeeded in bringing an end to harassment and illegal eviction. Both are still common, especially when there are resident landlords. The law itself must bear some considerable responsibility for failing to stamp out these activities. Enforcement has been desultory. The magistrates' courts, where these offences are commonly tried, have power to impose fines of up to £400, or to send offenders to prison for up to six months. In 1966, the average penalty for an offence of illegal eviction was a fine of only £22.50, and by the first six months of 1970, this had dropped to £15.75; over the same period, the average fines for harassment dropped from £20.50 to £16.75.

These pathetic penalties suggest that magistrates do not consider the offences to be very much worse than a breach of parking regulations. The spirit of the criminal law is to deter and to punish; where harassment and eviction are involved, the courts have effectively failed to do either. Because the penalties are so low, they gain little or no attention from even the local press and it is media attention which can be the most effective tool for impressing upon landlords that this sort of behaviour will not be tolerated by society as a whole.

Individual occupiers will in fact get much more help from the civil courts. There are limited circumstances in which the magistrates' courts can make an order for compensation, but it cannot order damages for suffering or inconvenience. The magistrates' court has no power to make an order compelling a landlord to readmit an evicted occupier, either immediately — which is when it will be most needed — or at all. Strictly, they cannot even order a landlord to cease harassing an occupier, although they can bind a landlord over to keep the peace, or they could discharge a landlord without punishment, conditional on no further offences being committed.

The position is very different indeed in the civil courts — the county courts and the High Court — where remedies are pursued between the parties. They have power to order a landlord to readmit an evicted occupier, and they can exercise this power so quickly that an occupier may be able to get back in the same day as an eviction, or, at least, the same day as he has sought advice. They can also make orders restraining further harassment or eviction. At the end of a case, civil courts can make permanent orders which remain in force indefinitely and breach of which would be a contempt of court. They can also order the landlord to pay the occupier for any actual loss suffered, and for distress, shock, suffering, etc.

A social worker who encounters a client who is being harassed, or who has been or is about to be illegally evicted, needs to know immediately what is possible in practice. The first thing to do will be to make contact with the local authority Tenancy Relations/Harassment Officer who may be able to conciliate between the parties and avert court proceedings. If this intervention is not successful, the social worker will need to know what possibilities there are for immediate civil action.

At the same time, it would be quite wrong to abandon the idea of criminal proceedings. To do this would be to fall victim to the courts' own indifference. Only by constantly impressing upon courts just how common harassment and illegal eviction still are, and by impressing upon them too just how distressing an incident can be to an occupier, is there any prospect at all either of pushing the courts into awarding punishment to fit the crime or, if the courts persist in refusing to treat the offences seriously, building up a case for legislative reform compelling the courts to do so.

The two approaches, civil and criminal, are wholly different. There are different procedures, in different courts, and the language and ideas of the two systems are also very different indeed. In the criminal courts, what is under examination is the behaviour of an individual in relation to what has been defined as an offence against society. In the civil courts, what is under examination is whether one party has offended the individual rights of another. The approaches must, therefore, be described separately:

1. *Criminal Proceedings*; and
2. *Civil Proceedings*.

1. *Criminal Proceedings*

The definitions of the criminal offences of illegal eviction and harassment are contained in the Protection From Eviction Act 1977, s. 1:

"(2) If any person unlawfully deprives the residential occupier of any premises of his occupation of the premises or any part thereof, or attempts to do so, he shall be guilty of an offence unless he proves that he believed, and had reasonable cause to believe, that the residential occupier had ceased to reside in the premises.

"(3) If any person with intent to cause the residential occupier of any premises —

(a) to give up occupation of the premises or any part thereof; or

(b) to refrain from exercising any right or pursuing any remedy in respect of the premises or part thereof;

does acts calculated to interfere with the peace or comfort of the residential occupier or members of his household, or persistently withdraws or withholds services reasonably required for the occupation of the premises as a residence, he shall be guilty of an offence."

There are several points which must now be considered in further detail:

(i) Meaning of residential occupier;
(ii) Acts of harassment;
(iii) Acts of eviction;
(iv) The accused;
(v) Criminal procedure;
(vi) The police;
(vii) Tenancy Relations/Harassment Officers;
(viii) Private prosecutions;
(ix) Penalties;
(x) Compensation.

(i) *Meaning of residential occupier*

This is also defined in section 1 of the Act:

"(1) In this section "residential occupier", in relation to any premises, means a person occupying the premises as a residence, whether under a contract or by virtue of any enactment or rule of law giving him the right to remain in occupation or restricting the right of any other person to recover possession of the premises."

Occupation as a residence is a question of fact, and common sense, not law. It is not necessary to show, for example, that the occupier had sufficient residence to sustain a claim to statutory tenancy (see Chapter 4, 2(i)). Obviously, someone who merely visits a friend is not residing in premises, not even if he stays overnight or, perhaps for a couple of nights. The same is no doubt true of a short-term hotel guest. But once a person begins to use premises to live in, in any normal sense of the expression, then the premises are being occupied as a residence. A person can have two residences, *e.g.* a student who lives away from home during the term-time will normally be considered resident both at home and at college. A person does not stop residing in premises just because, for example, he goes away for a holiday, or for some other reason is temporarily absent. The residence will continue during such breaks as if the occupier was actually present.

The definition of residential occupier is not free from complexity. But it can be restated without difficulty in terms which have been used in the earlier chapters of this book. *All* tenants and licensees (including service tenants and occupiers) whose tenancies and licences have *not* been brought to an end are residential occupiers because they are occupying under contract. It does not matter if the person harassing or evicting is not a party to the contract: what is in question is whether or not the occupier is a residential occupier. A leasehold owner-occupier is also occupying under contract and a freehold owner-occupier does so by "rule of law." Protected tenants whose contractual tenancies have been brought to an end and who occupy as statutory tenants (see Chapter 4) do so "by virtue of an enactment." *All other* former tenants are residential occupiers because there is an enactment "restricting the right of any other person to recover possession of the premises", the enactment is the Protection From Eviction Act itself, s. 3. Section 3 also protects former service occupiers who were granted some exclusive occupation of their accommodation under the employment arrangement, and anyone lawfully living with either such a service occupier or a former unprotected tenant at the end of the tenancy (or occupancy). This will apply even if the former tenant or service occupier has himself left the premises.

In addition, there are enactments restricting the right of another person to recover possession of premises which serve to protect deserted spouses and, in some cases, even trespassers. The Matrimonial Homes Act 1967 prohibits an owner or tenant-spouse from evicting a non-owner or non-tenant-spouse from the matrimonial home without an order of a court. Such an order will normally be made during the course of domestic proceedings and this subject is considered in the next Chapter. However, because there is *an* enactment which restricts the right of *some* other person, the deserted spouse qualifies as a residential occupier for the purposes of the Protection From Eviction Act, even if it is not the other spouse who is attempting to get him out. The criminal offence of violent entry for the purposes of eviction of a trespasser has been described in

Chapter 6. Insofar as a trespasser is protected from eviction by that provision, so also will he be protected from eviction under this Act.

The definition of residential occupier is, therefore, very wide indeed. It is possible to evict certain occupiers, *e.g.* trespassers, former licensees, without taking court proceedings, so long as the Criminal Law Act 1977 is not broken, so long as no other criminal offence is committed, so long as the licence is already at an end, so long as the occupier is indeed a former licensee and not a former tenant, so long as the former licensee was not living with a former tenant who was not a protected tenant, etc. This list of reservations itself should be sufficient to deter any landlord from seeking to recover possession without taking court proceedings, for the risk of committing an offence when doing so will otherwise be very high. It is for this reason that landlords are invariably advised — and well-advised — by lawyers to take court proceedings before evicting an occupier.

(ii) *Acts of harassment*

The words of the section are fairly easy to follow. Whatever is done must be done with one of the two sorts of appropriate intention. The most common intention is that of attempting to cause the occupier to give up possession of the premises or part of them, *e.g.* one room. But harassment also occurs with the other objective in mind, *e.g.* to try and deter an occupier from applying to the Rent Officer or Rent Tribunal, or to deter him from complaining to an Environmental Health Officer about the condition of the property.

The criminal action can also be committed in different ways: by persistently withholding or withdrawing services, such as gas and electricity, reasonably required for the occupation of the premises as a residence, *i.e.* more than just once or twice; or by doing acts, in the plural, which are calculated to interfere with the peace or comfort of the residential occupier or members of his household. This broad definition allows the law to catch odd actions which may not be obvious acts of harassment, such as hanging around a sensitive and perhaps elderly occupier, or coming into the premises so frequently that the occupier begins to feel that they are no longer his home.

Disconnection of utilities probably qualifies as the most common form of harassment. The necessary intention is often proved by shouted abuses and orders to get out, or by a notice to quit, whether valid or not. Refusing to allow an occupier the use of some facility or other, *e.g.* a bathroom or lavatory, is another common means of harassing someone. This commonly occurs when there is a resident landlord.

(iii) *Acts of eviction*

There are three points to note in connection with the definition of eviction:

(a) eviction can be from the whole or part of the premises in question;

(b) the offence is committed either by a successful eviction or by an attempted eviction; and

(c) the defence which is available to an accused requires him to show that he believed *and* had reasonable cause to believe that the residential occupier had ceased to reside in the premises. This means that a subjective, but unreasonable belief will not result in acquittal.

Eviction normally takes place when an occupier is out of the premises, either away for a few days or even just out shopping. Quite often, the occupier, or perhaps a spouse with children, will return to find that all the family's belongings have been put out on the street, the locks changed, none of the other occupiers are willing to "get involved," and the landlord and perhaps some of his friends are inside to prevent any attempt to get back in by force. It must be recognised that the occupier who returns home to find this sort of situation is likely to suffer from some degree of shock. He will need immediate comfort but, most of all, guidance on what to do. The quicker the occupier can be restored to the premises, the less the suffering will be. An eviction which takes place while the occupier is at home is also likely to be an offence by the landlord against the provisions restricting violent entry (Criminal Law Act 1977, s. 6, p. 121).

(iv) *The accused*

Anyone can be charged with either of these offences, not only a landlord or his friends or agents. It may, however, be difficult to establish the necessary intention for harassment unless the act is done by someone with connections with the landlord. On the face of it, no one else is likely to have the incentive to try and make the occupier get out. This does not mean that it is impossible to convict anyone other than the landlord or his cohorts, but it serves as a useful check on abuse of the section by squabbling neighbours before the trouble escalates to such a point where, as might eventually be the case, one neighbour is actively trying to make the other decamp. Once it reaches that pitch, even a neighbour might be committing an offence, most probably of harassment. A prospective future occupier may also have the necessary incentive and, consequently, the necessary intention. If the harassment or eviction is performed on behalf of a limited company, then a director or any officer of the company will also be guilty of an offence if he consented to or connived at the harassment, or it happened because of his negligence. In law, even a company can commit a criminal offence.

(v) *Criminal procedure*

Criminal proceedings are conducted in the magistrates' court. A prosecution may be initiated by an injured party, or, in cases of harassment and eviction, by a Tenancy Relations/ Harassment Officer. Unlike most other criminal matters, prosecutions are not brought by the police.

The first stage of a criminal action is that the prosecutor must attend before the magistrates for the area in which the offence happened and lay an information stating what the facts of the matter are. Provided that, on this account, it would appear that an offence has been committed, a summons will be issued and the accused will be obliged to appear at court on some future date.

On that appearance, the accused will be invited to plead guilty or not guilty to the offence. If he pleads guilty, the court will normally consider the penalty then and there. It may also consider any questions of compensation which are relevant.

If he pleads not guilty, it is usual for the case to be adjourned to another day when time will be set aside for the trial. The court is not obliged to do this, and could in theory commence the trial at once, but this will be very uncommon as magistrates' courts are extremely busy and do not usually have the time for a full trial on the same day. There may in fact be several such adjournments. This can often be disconcerting to an occupier/witness who may begin to wonder if the case will ever be heard and will also sometimes suspect that the adjournments indicate that the landlord "has something up his sleeve." Adjournments do not mean anything of the sort: they are perfectly normal occurrences.

The accused has a right to ask to be tried in the Crown Court, by a judge and jury. This is not often done as, if convicted, the accused stands to suffer more serious penalties and the costs of a Crown Court case can be prohibitive if legal aid has not been granted, *e.g.* because of a landlord's assets.

When the case actually comes on for hearing, it starts with an outline of the facts by the prosecution, which will then present its evidence to the court. It will be at this stage that any witnesses, including the occupier, will be called. The landlord or, if he is represented, his lawyer, will normally cross-examine each of the witnesses for the prosecution, including the occupier. When the prosecution case has closed, the defence calls its witnesses, who may be cross-examined by or on behalf of the prosecutor. The only closing speech is that of the defence. The magistrates will then consider, perhaps after retiring to talk it over between themselves, whether the offence has been proved beyond reasonable doubt or not, and will either convict or acquit. If they convict, they will decide the appropriate penalty and may also consider questions of compensation.

(vi) *The police*

There is nothing in the law to prevent the police from getting involved in cases of harassment and illegal eviction. They do not do so as a matter of policy. This they justify on the grounds of the complexity of the issues, *i.e.* the difficulty knowing whether someone is a residential occupier for the purposes of the Act or not. The police will, however, come to the scene of a serious harassment or an eviction, particularly if they have reason to believe that a breach of the peace may occur, or that there may be violence involved. They will, however, only arrest if some offence other than harassment or illegal eviction is involved.

They will also, of course, prosecute in such cases. A newspaper report in *The Times*, July 28, 1977, recounts how a landlord conducted a three-year campaign of terror designed to drive out his tenants. It culminated in him setting fire to the house while they were asleep. Four of the occupiers died. The landlord was convicted of manslaughter and sent to jail for 10 years. But until this tragic end, and the commission of the more serious crime, the police had refused to become involved despite complaints to them from a local Law Centre representing the occupiers.

When a police officer attends at the scene of an incident, he will keep a note of what happens and, in particular, what is said, *e.g.* an admission by the landlord that an occupier is a tenant. If he is not doing so, he should be asked to note anything of especial relevance as it will be possible in subsequent criminal or civil proceedings to call the officer as a witness. If the notes were made at the time of the incident, or as soon as possible afterwards, the officer will be permitted to read them out and this is usually considered highly reliable evidence. Anyone can make such a contemporaneous note and a social worker witnessing an incident should certainly do so. He will also be allowed to refer to them in court.

(vii) *Tenancy Relations/Harassment Officers*

All local authorities have power, which most of them use, to appoint special officers to deal with problems in the private sector of tenanted accommodation. They can prosecute landlord/tenant offences, including all of those described in this book, *e.g.* failure to provide rent book, failure to provide landlord's name and address (Chapter 2), demanding a premium or an illegal accommodation agency fee (Chapter 4), overcharging a Rent Tribunal rent (Chapter 5). These officers are called either Tenancy Relations or Harassment Officers and many of them belong to the Association of Tenancy Relations Officers.

In the event of any act of harassment or eviction, the Tenancy Relations/Harassment Officer should be contacted without delay. If it is urgent, he will normally call straight round to the premises and try and sort the problem out face to face with the landlord and the occupier. Some of them even have radio-linked cars. In addition or, if the matter is not urgent, in the alternative, he may write to the landlord, warning him of the possible offences and penalties, and inviting comment.

The Tenancy Relations/Harassment Officer does not usually make prosecution the goal of his job. The officers work by way of conciliation, reinforced with the possibility of prosecution. This will often be no more than a slim possibility, but many landlords will not know this. A Tenancy Relations/Harassment Officer cannot normally decide on his own initiative to prosecute: the prosecution will be handled by the local authority's legal department. Many of these legal departments adopt a somewhat less than fervent attitude to such prosecutions, in effect reflecting the attitudes of the courts. The attitudes of individual Tenancy Relations/Harassment officers can range from those who consider they have failed in their work whenever they are forced into prosecuting, to those who cannot see why a person who has committed a criminal offence should not be prosecuted, like any other criminal. It may, perhaps, not be irrelevant to remark that there are many ex-police officers in these posts.

One complaint which the officers often voice is that they do not receive sufficient support from occupiers themselves at later proceedings. Some may, of course, still be living in the same premises and for that reason might be unwilling to testify against their landlords; others may have left and not bothered to remain in touch with the prosecuting officer. It is understandable that an occupier should take this attitude, but it is clearly to be regretted that the circumstances described in these paragraphs combine to make harassment and eviction cases comparatively rare. This is another factor which affects the almost frivolous attitude of the courts.

(viii) *Private prosecutions*

If the Tenancy Relations/Harassment Officer will not prosecute, then it is still open to the individual occupier who has been harassed or illegally evicted to do so. Legal aid will not be available for a prosecution, although legal advice could be sought beforehand: see Appendix 2. The assistance of one of the agencies referred to in Appendix 2 might also result in free representation, which should certainly be used if available.

If the occupier does proceed on his own, he should take care always to have his witnesses and any documentary supporting evidence at court for the day of the full hearing. If there is any doubt as to whether the trial will take place on a particular day, then he should check with the clerk of the court beforehand.

Understandably, not many occupiers are prepared to shoulder the heavy responsibility of a private prosecution unassisted and run the risk of having to pay the landlord's costs if he is acquitted.

(ix) *Penalties*

The penalties in the magistrates' court have already been described: in theory, the court can order a fine of up to £400, or can impose six months imprisonment, or both, although it rarely does more than force the landlord to pay a small fine. If the landlord elects trial in the Crown Court, then he could be fined up to an unlimited amount, or sent to prison for up to two years, or both, although, again, rarely if ever are these maximum penalties applied or even approached.

(x) *Compensation*

Either sort of court has power to award compensation for "personal injury, loss or damage resulting from (an) offence," (Powers of Criminal Courts Act 1973, s. 35). This power is not frequently used. This may be because when a local authority prosecutes, it is not doing so strictly on behalf of or in the interests of the particular occupier, but in discharge of its public duties.

The powers are only used in relation to ascertainable loss, such as damaged property, time off work through injury, cost of overnight accommodation or eating out, etc. It is not available for shock, distress, inconvenience or discomfort. Nor, in the case of illegal eviction, could it be used for loss of the home itself as this does not have an easily identified value. But even though courts do not use these powers frequently, and may even be unfamiliar with them they can and should be asked to order compensation where this would avoid the necessity to commence a wholly new set of proceedings, in the civil courts. A local authority lawyer who is prosecuting can be asked to apply on behalf of the occupier. Any documentary evidence of loss sustained by the occupier, such as bills, should be brought to court.

2. *Civil Proceedings*

The usual way in which a civil action is started is considered in Appendix 1. In this Chapter we are only concerned with so much of civil procedure as is especially relevant to harassment and illegal eviction.

Civil proceedings are brought in either the county court, usually for the area in which the incident happens, or in the High Court. The High Court has the fullest civil jurisdiction of all, but the county court has only limited powers. Most cases of harassment and illegal eviction will be brought in the county courts, unless the amount of damages (monetary compensation) claimed is particularly high.

The civil remedies which may be awarded by either sort of court are:

(i) Injunctions; and
(ii) Damages.

There are further remedies which are not normally applicable to cases of harassment and illegal eviction: see Appendix 1.

(i) *Injunctions*

An injunction is an order of the court. It will always identify the person, or persons, who is or are to be bound by it. Failure to comply with the terms of an injunction is a contempt of court. Contempt can be punished by either a fine or imprisonment. It is uncommon for civil courts to send a landlord who is in breach of an injunction to prison, unless he persists in his refusal to obey it.

An injunction is normally awarded as part of the judgment at the end of the case. This is called a "final order." A civil case, even in the county court, can take many months to be heard. There are many stages of pre-trial procedure to be followed, there may be requests for adjournments because one side or the other is not ready for trial, and the court will have to find time to fit the case in.

What an occupier who has been harassed or illegally evicted wants is an immediate order. Sometimes, a matter is so urgent that it cannot even be left for the few days necessary to give the other side an opportunity to attend court. In cases of such urgency, the court will grant an *ex parte* order, *i.e.* one that is based upon the unchallenged evidence of the occupier only. This is normally produced in court by affidavit, *i.e.* a sworn statement.

The courts will only use their powers to make ex parte orders if there has been little or no delay before they are asked to do so. A harassment must be quite serious, for example, disconnection of utilities, before a court will make an order either compelling the landlord to restore the utilities or restraining any further harassment, on an *ex parte* hearing. An illegal eviction will normally be considered sufficiently urgent, especially if the person evicted has nowhere else to stay, or nowhere else that is satisfactory, but the courts will not grant an *ex parte* order if there has been any unnecessary delay before it is asked to do so. An ex parte order should always be sought immediately.

If an order is granted *ex parte*, it will usually be for only a few days or a week, until a further hearing when the court will listen to the other side of the case and decide whether or not the order should be continued until the full trial of the matter. If a matter is not serious enough to merit an *ex parte* order, then the matter does not have to be left until the full trial: there can still be an application for a hearing within a few days or a week. This sort of hearing is called an *inter partes* hearing, *i.e.* one between both parties. Orders made at either an *ex parte* or an inter partes hearing are called interim injunctions, or orders, to distinguish them from final injunctions, or orders, which are only made at the end of the case.

When a judge is deciding whether or not to grant an interim injunction, he does not decide the full merits of the case. The judge does not decide which side is telling the truth, or which side is in the right. He only decides what order should be made, pending the full trial, on a *balance of convenience*. Unless premises have already been re-occupied by someone else, or by the landlord himself, the balance of convenience will almost always be in the occupier's favour, although it may be subject to an undertaking by the occupier to pay the rent pending the trial. The balance of convenience will also almost invariably be with the occupier where harassment is in issue.

Although the issue is one of balance of convenience, the strength of a case will still affect the decision of the court, for otherwise a complete stranger might wander into a court and allege that he has been evicted from an empty property, simply to gain a right of occupation for the few months pending trial. If the occupier's case is a strong one, on the face of it, then even if the landlord has relet the premises, or if the landlord is himself in occupation, the court will be very reluctant indeed to allow the landlord to benefit from what appears to be both the commission of a criminal offence and a very serious breach of the civil law, by allowing him to remain in occupation until trial. The court will instead be inclined to grant the occupier's request for an immediate order. The strength of a case is measured not solely by reference to what evidence the occupier offers, but also by what sort of reply the landlord makes. At an inter partes hearing, the landlord is likely to file an answer, also by way of affidavit, to the occupier's claim.

(ii) *Damages*

Damages are not awarded until the end of the case. It is, nonetheless, important to consider them, even if not in great detail, at the outset, because this might affect which of the two civil courts the action is brought in. Shortly, the county court only has power to grant damages up to £2000. But the loss of a protected tenancy of a whole house, or even possibly a flat, in, at least, London, and possibly the centres of some of the other major cities, may well be worth this sort of money. It may also be that the occupier has lost property in excess of that sum, for example, if his property was dumped outside the premises and stolen. The total damages claimed must not exceed £2000 if the claim is to remain within the jurisdiction of the county court.

There are several different sorts of damages. A person claims *special* damages for specific sums of money, *e.g.* damages to furniture, cost of eating out or overnight accommodation, lost property, etc. These are the same sorts of damages which may be claimed in the magistrates' courts as compensation. *General* damages are unquantified sums which are claimed in respect of, for example, suffering, shock, distress, physical injury, inconvenience, the lost right of occupation itself or any other harm to which a specific value cannot be attached, *e.g.* additional electricity costs because gas is cut off. *Aggravated* damages are awarded where the manner of that which is being sued for was especially mean, unpleasant, brutal, etc. *Exemplary* damages are awarded where it would appear that the landlord has, for example evicted a tenant, calculating to himself that any profit made, for example from sale of the property with vacant possession, will be more than any damages awarded against him. In other words, that he can make a profit, even out of doing something wrong. In *Cassell* v. *Broome*, the House of Lords considered the question of exemplary damages and Lord Hailsham, LC, said:

> "How, it may be asked, about the late Mr. Rachman, who is alleged to have used hired bullies to intimidate statutory tenants by violence or threats of violence into giving up vacant possession of their residences and so placing a valuable asset in the hands of the landlord? My answer must be that if this is not a cynical calculation of profit and cold-blooded disregard of a plaintiff's rights, I do not know what is ... "

And in the recent case of *Drane* v. *Evangelou*, Lord Justice Lawton said that to deprive a tenant of a roof over his head was one of the worst torts (wrongs) that could be committed. It brought the law into disrespect. He also expressed his surprise

that the landlord had not been prosecuted under what is now
s. 1 of the Protection From Eviction Act, 1977. Lord Denning,
MR, applied the words of an earlier case: "Exemplary
damages can properly be awarded whenever it is necessary to
teach a wrongdoer that tort does not pay."

The High Court can award an injunction and/or damages
to an unlimited amount in any civil action. The county court
can normally only award an injunction if the plaintiff has
made a claim for damages within its jurisdiction, £2000, at the
same time. Once the claim has been made then, of course, it
has the power to grant an interim injunction at an early stage
in the proceedings, even though it will not finally decide
whether to award a full injunction and/or damages, nor how
much damages it will award, until the end of the trial.
However, the county court has an additional and separate
power, under the *Administration of Justice Act 1977, s. 14*,
which inserted a new section, *s. 51A*, in *the County Courts Act
1959*, to grant an injunction even though no claim for
damages has been made, in any case in which possession,
occupation, use or enjoyment of land is in issue, *i.e.* harassment and illegal eviction. This claim may be made where the
only real redress the occupier is seeking is the injunction, and a
claim for damages would not be well founded, for example
because the injunction was to prevent an eviction and no harm
had yet occurred, or because an interim injunction would be
awarded so quickly that no loss or suffering had yet taken place
and the occupier was of a sufficient robust character not really
to have suffered shock or distress.

Injunctions may be granted whenever whatever wrong has
been done can be rectified by an order, or else in order to
prevent a wrong being committed. Damages are awarded
when there has been actual loss as a result of a wrong, even if
only of the order of suffering, shock, distress, etc., although in
some cases the law will assume that the act itself is injury
enough to sustain a claim for damages in money, *e.g.* trespass.

Neither the county court nor the High Court can make any
order at all, however, until an action has been commenced: see
Appendix 1. Legal aid will be available for a civil action based
on harassment or illegal eviction: see Appendix 2. In order to
commence an action in a civil court, it is necessary to show

that the plaintiff has what is known as a cause of action. A court does not have power to make an order because, for example, you do not like the colour of your neighbour's hair, or because someone jumps in front of you in a bus queue, or because another person calls you a silly idiot. On the other hand, there will be a cause of action if your neighbour plays music so loudly or at anti-social hours that he disturbs your enjoyment of your own home, or if the queue-jumper used so much force that he assaulted you, or if what was said was of a defamatory character.

All of these causes of action are known as "torts," or civil wrongs. A tort is an action which the law recognises is wrongful for one person, who is the person complained about, to do to the person complaining. There are several torts which may be used in connection with harassment and illegal eviction. In addition, there is always a cause of action when one party breaks a contract with another, whether completely or in a material particular. Breach of contract will also often be appropriate to cases of harassment and illegal eviction.

In considering civil proceedings for harassment and illegal eviction, one must use the language and terminology of the civil courts. There is no cause of action known simply as harassment or illegal eviction. Nor can an individual sue just because a criminal offence of harassment or illegal eviction has been committed: *McCall* v. *Abelesz*. Instead, the activities which are described in the criminal law as harassment and illegal eviction must be redefined in the language of causes of action known to the civil law.

(a) Breach of contract

Both tenancy and licence are contracts. A licensee may sue for breach of contract or breach of a term of the contract. A term of a contract may actually be stated, or it may be implied, if it is a necessary term to make the contract meaningful, for example a contract for occupation as a residence would not be very meaningful if there was no term at least implied that during the subsistence of the contract the landlord would ensure that there was a supply of gas and electricity to the premises, for lighting and perhaps cooking. This does not mean that the licensee need not pay for the gas or electricity, even by way of coin meter, but that it is the landlord's responsibility to ensure that it is available for the occupier's use.

A similar term will be implied, if not actually expressed, into a contract of tenancy. In addition, into every tenancy there is implied, again, unless it is actually expressed, a promise by the landlord that the tenant will have the "quiet enjoyment" of the premises so long as the tenancy shall last. In *Kenny* v. *Preen*, it was said that the promise was broken by an act which was an invasion of the right of the tenant to remain in possession undisturbed. Clearly, this includes an actual or threatened eviction, and almost every act of harassment. In *McCall* v. *Abelesz*, disconnection of utilities was described as both a breach of implied term, and as an interference with quiet enjoyment. Any conduct by a landlord which interferes with the tenant's freedom of action in exercising his rights as tenant will be an interference with the covenant for quiet enjoyment.

Both restricted tenancy and restricted licence last so long as any Rent Tribunal security of tenure is in force (see Chap. 5) and these causes of action can also be used by a statutory tenant (see Chapter 4), even after the end of the contractual tenancy. They can, obviously, be used by all tenants and contractual licensees until the tenancy or licence is brought properly to an end. However, as these causes of action are contractual, they can only be used against another party to a contract, *i.e.* the landlord. A landlord will be responsible for his own actions, and those done on his behalf, *e.g.* by an agent.

(b) Breach of statutory duty

All of the legislation described in this book is of a class of legislation which is commonly described as protective, i.e. intended to protect some class of the population or other. There are many such legislative provisions. Sometimes, legislation imposes a duty on an individual, or on a public body, and sometimes it reinforces this duty with criminal sanctions. Regardless of whether or not the duty is reinforced with criminal sanctions, some protective legislation is considered by the courts to create a right, on the part of the person who is to be protected by it, to sue the person on whom the duty is imposed. This, for example, has been held to apply where there has been a breach of fire precautions on the part of a landlord (*Solomon* v. *Gertzenstein.*) In *McCall* v. *Abelesz*, it was held that this is *not* so in the cases of harassment and illegal eviction. In *Warder* v. *Cooper*, however, the court decided that someone evicted in breach of what is now s. 3 of the Protection From Eviction Act 1977, can sue the landlord. Section 3 requires a landlord to take court proceedings before evicting any former unprotected tenant, or a service occupier who had exclusive occupation of his premises, or anyone lawfully living with either such class at the time the right of occupation was brought to an end. The distinction is that there is no direct criminal sanction attached to s. 3, although, of course, a breach of s. 3 would also be a breach of s. 1 and, as such, a criminal offence. This class of action is known as breach of statutory duty.

Breach of statutory duty is a tort, but the only person who can be sued is the landlord as the section itself only places a duty to take court proceedings on the landlord. The landlord will also be liable for an eviction carried out on his behalf. The cause of action will arise only in respect of eviction or, if an injunction only is sought, an attempted eviction.

(c) Trespass to land

Once there is a tenancy, the tenant has possession of the premises, to the exclusion of all others, including the landlord. A landlord can, therefore, trespass on the premises of his own tenant. There is some legal authority for the proposition that the sort of exclusive occupation which most licensees have is enough possession for the purposes of trespass. This is because it is possession in fact, rather than legally defined possession, which matters.

A person is a trespasser whenever he enters the land or premises of another without permission. It is also a trespass to place anything on someone else's property without permission. In one case, it was held to be a trespass to drive a nail into someone else's wall, which, by analogy, would apply to a

landlord who nails up a door or blocks up a lock. A person is
also a trespasser if he has permission to be on someone's
premises for one purpose but uses it for another. For example,
a landlord calling around to collect the rent or inspect for
repairs will become a trespasser if he uses the occasion to
abuse, threaten or harass the occupier. Similarly, a person
given permission to enter must leave once he is asked to do so
and, once a reasonable time has been given for the exit,
becomes a trespasser. Reasonable time here, as with residential
licence, is reasonable in all the circumstances and, where a
person is just visiting, will be a matter of however long it would
normally take to get to the door.

Trespass is a tort and anyone who trespasses can be sued for
it. A landlord is liable for the torts of his agents, if the torts
were committed with his approval or on his behalf. An evicted
or harassed occupier can sue the landlord and, if the landlord
got someone else to do his dirty work, that person as well.

(d) Assault

Harassment and eviction will often be accompanies by
assaults. An assault is not necessarily a directly physical act. It
may be no more than some gesture which suggests that the
person to whom it is made is about to be attacked physically.
Threatening words on their own are not an assault, and it is
difficult to prove unless there has been some sort of physical
attack, although this might be with a weapon, piece of
furniture, or merely by shoving an occupier around. An
assault is a tort and the remarks in the last paragraph will,
therefore, apply in the same way to assault.

(e) Nuisance

Like trespass, this is a cause of action which can be used by
someone in possession of land, which certainly includes a
tenant and may include a licensee. A nuisance is anything
which interferes with the reasonable use and enjoyment of
property, *e.g.* noise, smells, even hanging about outside someone's home. Most acts of harassment will constitute a nuisance,
although this may not be so if the act is negative, *e.g.* a with-
drawal of services. Nuisance is also a tort.

(f) Trespass to goods

Any direct interference with another person's belongings is a trespass to goods. If belongings are actually removed, this may also be conversion. Conversion is the act of dealing with someone else's property in any manner that is inconsistent with the right of the other person to possession of it. Trespass to goods and conversion are torts.

Further Reading

"Quiet Enjoyment? The Law, Practice and Procedure in Harassment and Illegal Eviction," Andrew Arden and Martin Partington, Legal Action Group.

9 Breakup of Relationship

In this Chapter, we shall consider the law as it relates to housing on the breakup of a relationship. This is, to some extent, an artificial study, because decisions cannot and will not be taken on the basis of housing law, or law itself, alone. There will be many other considerations to bring to bear, including that of the emotional desirability of exercising particular rights. The social worker in practice cannot, in any event, do more than offer to a client in this situation the range of options that are open to him.

In recent years, there have been many developments in relation to domestic affairs and, especially, in relation to the property rights of wives. The courts and Parliament have come to realise the unequal position of women in a cohabitation relationship, much as it has been recognised in other areas, *e.g.* the Equal Pay Act 1970, and the Sex Discrimination Act 1975. There has been legislation to deal with the subject, especially the Matrimonial Homes Act 1967, the Matrimonial Causes Act 1973, and the Domestic Violence and Matrimonial Proceedings Act 1976. In addition, the common law has continued to develop the long-standing concept of "trusts" as it relates to rights between cohabiting partners.

In this Chapter, we shall consider:

1. *The Common Law*:
2. *The Married Women's Property Act 1882*;
3. *The Matrimonial Homes Act 1967*;
4. *The Matrimonial Causes Act 1973*;
5. *The Domestic Violence Act 1976*; and
6. *Further Considerations*.

None of these Acts or laws are mutually exclusive: it will be common for provisions contained in more than one Act to apply in the same case. In addition, the courts have a fairly broad discretion to make such orders as are considered appropriate at any stage in the proceedings: interim orders (see Chap. 8) are very commonplace, to the point of being the norm.

1. *The Common Law*

The common law doctrine of trust applies in a cohabitation relationship, as much as it can apply to any appropriate situation. This doctrine deals with the position which arises at law whenever property is held in the name of one person, but is intended for the benefit of another. Indeed, a person can also hold property in his name, not for the benefit of another individual, but for the benefit of a cause or purpose, *e.g.* a charity. This would also be a trust.

Property held on trust must be used for the purposes for which it was intended. Some people leave property on trust in their wills, for example a large family estate may be left on trust so as to ensure that beneficiaries under the will can have the benefit and use of the property for their lifetimes, but cannot actually dispose of it.

Property can be held on trust for the benefit of a number of individuals, including one of the trustees himself. A man, for example, could buy a house, and put it on trust for the use of himself and his wife and/or children. The man could not subsequently dispose of the property, unless all the beneficiaries consented to the proposed arrangements.

Property is automatically considered to be held on trust whenever two or more people own land or premises jointly. This is a particular type of trust: a trust for sale. The effect of a trust for sale is that any of the joint owners can actually force the property to be sold, even against the wishes of the other party. This is an obviously necessary provision, for the value of a half-share in a house will be nugatory if it is not possible to force a sale at will.

Whenever property is held on trust, or is alleged to be held on trust, the High Court has power to declare whether or not it is held on trust, and in what proportions or for whose benefit, and can also make orders which affect what should happen to the property in question.

Whenever property is held on trust, or is alleged to be held on trust, the High Court has power to declare whether or not it is held on trust, and in what proportions or for whose benefit, and can also make orders which affect what should happen to the property in question.

A trust sometimes arises under a formal deed. It may also arise if one person buys property, but for the benefit of another. It will also arise if one person buys property either wholly or in part with someone else's money. In the case of a house or flat, this might arise because, for example, a woman has put up all or part of the purchase price of the property, or all or part of the deposit on a property purchased under mortgage, or has simply contributed to the mortgage repayments, or even if she has contributed to maintenance or improvement of the property in such a way as to increase its value.

It follows that if a woman, whether or not married to a man, has made such a contribution, the law has power to intervene at a time of breakup, and make the appropriate declaration: for example, that the house is held for the benefit of the woman, or that she has a proportionate interest in it. These rights exist independently of the legislation described below and it will not normally be necessary for a wife to use them in relation to a husband. They may, however, be relevant in the case of a woman who has been cohabiting with a man without being married to him.

In *Cooke* v. *Head*, a couple who were not married bought a plot of land together. They had lived together for some time and always intended to marry once the man got a divorce. The property was in his name but they both worked and their joint incomes were used to pay the mortgage instalments and other outgoings on the property. This alone would have entitled the women to a share of the property. In addition, however, they themselves actually constructed a house on the land they had bought and the woman did a great deal of manual labour in the course of the construction work. Although her financial contributions only amounted to one-twelfth of the purchase price, she was held to be entitled to one-third, because of the additional work she had put in, which had contributed to the value of the property.

In *Eves* v. *Eves*, both parties were married to other people, but the woman changed her name by deed poll and the couple had two children together. The man deceived the woman into thinking that she was too young for her name to be put on the deeds of the house with his, and so it was bought in his name alone. The woman did a lot of work in the property, such as stripping wallpaper, painting, breaking up the concrete patio in the front and carting the rubble away to a skip. Together, the couple demolished a garden shed and built a new one. The relationship, however, broke up and the man took up with a new partner. The magistrates' court made a maintenance order in respect of the children, but the man moved his new partner into the house and became so threatening towards the woman that she and the children had to leave. The court decided that she was entitled to a one-quarter share of the property.

These provisions will normally only be relevant in the case of owner-occupied property. In theory, a woman could claim that a man had taken a tenancy for her benefit and the courts would have power to declare that she was therefore entitled to the benefit of it, which would mean the right to occupy under it. In the absence of extremely strong evidence, however, that the man was only taking the tenancy for her benefit, it is unlikely that the courts would exercise this power, especially as it would affect the position of a third party, the landlord. There would have to be sufficient evidence that the tenancy was taken for her benefit alone, for otherwise she would not have exclusive use of the premises and anything less will be of no value to her. This situation, however, is affected by the Domestic Violence Act where violence or the threat of violence is involved.

2. *The Married Women's Property Act 1882*

The provisions described below are, with the exception of the Domestic Violence Act, exclusively concerned with the courts' powers on breakup of a marriage. These powers can only be exercised during the course of matrimonial proceedings, or before the marriage breaks up. Once there is a decree absolute, the court will no longer have power to use the relevant provisions.

This is not the case where s. 17 of the Married Women's

Property Act is concerned. This gives a court power to make a declaration as to who really owns or has the benefit of property which has been held in one name of the party to a marriage. It can also make orders dealing with the property. The Act is applicable to people who are or who have been married, and also to those who, at the time the property in question was acquired, were intending to marry. The court's power arises on acquisition of the property and can be used at any time thereafter, whether or not the parties actually do get married, or even during the course of a marriage, or after the marriage is over, even when a decree has been made absolute.

Its main use is now in connection with those who have failed to take or receive sound advice at the time when matrimonial proceedings are going through. A woman may, for example, consent to a divorce without taking the correct steps to protect her position in relation to the home. If there has been some direct contribution, common law trust will still be available. In many cases, however, there will be no such direct contribution and the woman's entitlement to a share of the matrimonial property will be based instead on the principles described in 4, below. These principles will apply whether an application is made in the course of matrimonial proceedings, or whether the application is made under s. 17.

As with common law trust, its main use is in relation to owner-occupied property. There will be a similar reluctance on the part of a court to make a declaration where the property is only occupied under tenancy, although this is not impossible. The section cannot be used in relation to a licence. If a tenancy is still contractual and there is no prohibition in its terms against assignment, a court might use its s. 17 powers if it was satisfied that the tenancy was taken solely or principally for the benefit of the woman. Special provisions apply during the course of a marriage, and there are also special provisions for the transfer of protected tenancies: see 3, below.

3. *The Matrimonial Homes Act 1967*

The Matrimonial Homes Act 1967 contains two important provisions:

(a) Regardless of whether occupation is owner-occupation,

tenancy or contractual licence, one party to a marriage cannot exclude another from occupation of the matrimonial home without an order of the court. This order will normally be made in the course of matrimonial proceedings dealing with a number of considerations, but it could be made on application under this Act alone. The court also has power to make an order permitting a spouse who has been wrongfully evicted or excluded from the matrimonial home to re-enter. The court can make the order in respect of part only of the premises, *e.g.* excluding a husband from the residential part of the premises but allowing him to carry on his business in another part.

When someone who is not the owner-occupier, tenant or contractual licensee takes over mortgage or rent payments under these provisions, the landlord or mortgage company is obliged to accept them as if they were made by the owner-occupier, tenant or licensee. The court will exercise its powers to order one party to leave the matrimonial home whenever it is "fair, just and reasonable" to do so (*Walker* v. *Walker*) and will bear in mind the conduct of the parties generally, their respective needs and financial resources, the needs of any children of the marriage, and all the circumstances of the case.

A spouse who is not named on the deeds of a house or flat has a right of occupation under these provisions which he is entitled to register with the Land Charges Registry. The effect of this is that if the house is sold, the purchaser buys it subject to his right of occupation and is deemed to have known that he was and can remain in occupation. This is to prevent, for example, a husband selling the home over the head of a wife, before a court has an opportunity to make any order for transfer.

(b) Under s. 7 of the Act, the court also has power to order the transfer of a *protected* tenancy, whether contractual or statutory, from the name of one spouse into the name of another. This is so whether or not there is a prohibition on assignment in the terms of the tenancy agreement. Like the preceding provisions, this power can only be used before the marriage has come to an end, which will be on decree absolute. It is essential that the request to the court to exercise this power is made during the course of divorce proceedings, whether or not the divorce is a consent divorce.

4. *The Matrimonial Causes Act 1973*

It is this Act which contains the broad powers which a court now has to divide up matrimonial property when a marriage is in the course of being broken up. Like the Matrimonial Homes Act provisions, (3, above,) these powers are only exercisable between married partners, and they must be exercised before a divorce becomes final, *i.e.* decree absolute. These powers are exercised during the course of divorce or nullity proceedings. The court has power to apportion property between the parties and, if necessary, to order that property be transferred from the name of one party to that of another.

At one time, a wife who did not work and who had not contributed financially to the value of the property was not entitled as of right to any share in the property when the marriage broke up. She had to rely on the common law provisions, if there was any direct financial contribution, and this was so whether proceedings were taken at common law or under s. 17, Married Women's Property Act 1882. She might, of course, have been entitled to maintenance, and there may have been a settlement which took the form of a transfer of ownership of the matrimonial home. Alternatively, property might be transferred into her name but for the benefit of children of the marriage, in which case she would become the trustee of it herself, but only the trustee.

Over the years, however, the courts have come to recognise that the contribution of the non-earning spouse cannot be measured purely in terms of direct financial contribution. For a husband's earning power is clearly enhanced, not to say liberated, by the provision of domestic services by the wife who remains at home, including but not exclusively those involved in care of the children. Similarly, the courts have come to recognise that a woman should not live with and be dependent upon her husband for a period of time and suddenly be discarded by him without any further provision for her accommodation or support.

In *Wachtel* v. *Wachtel*, the Court of Appeal considered the correct principles to be applied to the division of property on breakdown of marriage. The courts start with a presumption that the wife, if the property is in the name of the husband alone, is entitled to one-third of its value. The property in question is not only house property, but all the property acquired on behalf of the marriage. Furthermore, other circumstances may dictate that a higher proportion is appropriate, for example, where the woman has in fact contributed more than a third financially, or, perhaps, because she has done so much work about the property that she is clearly entitled to more than a third, or because the man's behaviour has been so bad that it seems inequitable to leave the wife at the end of the marriage with the smaller proportion of the property.

In *Jones* v. *Jones*, the husband's behaviour was so appalling that he was eventually sent to prison for three years for grievous bodily harm towards his wife. Her injuries resulted in 75 per cent. disability of her right hand for life. In the event, the property was transferred in its entirety into the wife's name. A larger proportion than one-third might also be awarded where a husband has persistently failed or refused to pay maintenance, or because there are so many children, or because for some other reason the wife has some unusual need for a greater share, or else because, after a marriage of some years, an award of one-third will still leave the wife in no position to obtain a home for herself.

These rights, too, are mainly of interest only to owner-occupiers. A court can, however, order the transfer of a tenancy under these provisions, *Hale* v. *Hale*, regardless of whether the tenancy is protected or not. But it seems likely that this will only be possible if there is no provision in the tenancy agreement prohibiting assignment. This power could only be used during the contractual tenancy: there is nothing to transfer once it has come to an end, other than in the case of a statutory tenancy, which is dealt with under different provisions (see 3, above). The powers could not be used in connection with a licence, however, as a licence does not constitute the sort of property which the court can transfer: a licence is a personal right, while tenancy is a form of property.

5. *Domestic Violence Act 1976*

The provisions described above are designed to deal with what society has always considered to be of paramount importance, that is to say, they are provisions relating primarily to property rights. Divorce and trust procedures are cumbersome. They are ill-equipped to deal with immediate problems. In particular, they have proved to be inadequate to cope with the serious social problem of battered women. It may be remarked that the problem of battered women, and the property priority are not unrelated. Conventional male attitudes still show a marked tendency to consider wives, or other women with whom men may be living, as property themselves. In particular, it has always been an acceptable tenet of masculine domination that a man can do what he will to "his" woman, even to the extent of physical violence.

In recent years, this subject has gained considerable media attention. Refuges have been provided for battered women. Women's spokespersons have pressed for equal rights with men and, in common with other legislation designed to defeat historical iniquities, this has involved legislation designed to protect women from male behaviour.

Until the Domestic Violence Act came into force on June 1, 1977, the choices open to a woman being battered by a man with whom she was living were comparatively few. A married woman could commence divorce proceedings, in the course of which she could obtain an injunction compelling her husband to leave the matrimonial home, whether or not it was in his name alone, or in their joint names: see 3, above. But divorce proceedings are complex and awkward to launch, and cannot be brought in every civil court: see 6, below. Furthermore, many women did not actually want a divorce, despite violence, but sought only the immediate protection of the law. It was considered inappropriate that a woman should be confronted with the limited choices of either a full divorce, or no protection at all.

Cohabiting women were in a different position. They could not, of course, sue for divorce. They could make a claim for assault, in the county court, but to do this they would need to attach a claim for damages in order to bring the matter within the county court jurisdiction: see Appendix 1. Furthermore, this could not be used as a way of getting a man out of the home, if the home was in the man's name, or even if the couple's joint names. In that situation, the woman herself would have to leave, possibly to be confronted with homelessness and an unsympathetic local authority.

The Domestic Violence Act is available whenever one partner seeks the protection of the court against violence from the other. The protection is that of an injunction: see Chapter 8. A person can seek an injunction whenever a situation can be remedied by a court order, or whenever something that is wrong can be prevented by the order. It follows that the court's jurisdiction under this Act arises whenever there is either actual violence, or the mere threat of violence.

The court has power to make an order preventing one person molesting another, or molesting children living with that other, or ordering one partner to leave the domestic home, or ordering a person to readmit an excluded partner into the domestic home. An application to the court for one or more of these orders may be made by a spouse, or anyone who has been living together with the person from whom protection is sought as man and wife. Cohabiting couples can, therefore, use the Act.

The court has an additional power, to "back" the injunction for arrest. This means that a police officer can arrest without warrant any person whom he suspects is in breach of an order under the Act. The person must be brought back before the judge within 24 hours. This provision was necessary because the police have traditionally shown a marked reluctance to get involved in domestic disputes, even where they are informed that a woman is being subjected to severe maltreatment.

Unfortunately, the courts do not often use this power to "back for arrest." They fear an increase in their workload, particularly if an arrest is made at the beginning of the weekend, and the man has to be brought back before a judge within 24 hours in the normal way. The police, too, are unenthusiastic about these new duties. Both judges and police are undoubtedly still affected by the traditional male perspective.

The right to exclude one partner from the domestic home extends to cover the violent partner, even if he is the owner-occupier, tenant or contractual licensee. The provisions do not assist trespassers or bare licensees, although in the latter case, the same effect — exclusion from the home — could be achieved at the instigation of the person the couple is living with.

For some time it was thought that the provisions would not apply if, for example, the man was either the owner-occupier or the tenant, or even if he was a joint owner or joint tenant. The Court of Appeal held, in two cases, that the Act did not override fundamental property rights and, of course, at common law, one joint owner or tenant cannot exclude another. An injunction could still be granted in the course of matrimonial proceedings, because there is express provision, see 3 and 4, above, which clearly does override property rights. The Court of Appeal was not prepared to interpret the new Act in the same way.

In *Johnson* v. *Davies*, however, the Court of Appeal over-ruled its own previous decisions and stated quite clearly that the spirit and intention of the Act was to ensure that a battered woman could simultaneously remain in the domestic home and exclude the violent male, regardless of whether or not he had any property interests in the home. This decision was upheld by the House of Lords although the higher court did not agree with the method the Court of Appeal chose to reach its decision. *i.e.* it did not agree that the Court of Appeal had power to overrule its own earlier decisions. The injunction is, however, a short-term remedy and will not create an indefinite right of occupation. For example, where property is in the name of a male partner of a cohabiting couple, he can still terminate the woman's licence by reasonable notice and may thus be able to evict her with court proceedings *e.g.* Order 26 or 113: see Chapter 6.

Domestic Violence Act proceedings are very quick indeed. An application is made to the court, setting out the record of violence, and the court can and will hear an application ex parte in most cases. In almost every case it is likely that there will only be one or two subsequent inter partes hearings, and that it will not be necessary for there to be a full trial at some later date.

6. *Further Considerations*

(i) *Which Court?*

All matrimonial proceedings have to be brought in a properly accredited court. The High Court has power to conduct matrimonial proceedings which means, in London, the Family Division of the High Court, and in other cities where the High Court sits, the case will be brought in the Divorce Registry. However, some county courts also have power to hear matrimonial disputes, provided that they have been listed as a divorce county court. Domestic Violence Act proceedings can be brought in *any* county court or in the High Court, either as the sole basis for an action, or in conjunction with matrimonial proceedings. Matrimonial proceedings will customarily involve several of the remedies referred to in this Chapter.

(ii) *Procedures*

Civil procedure is described generally in Appendix 1. The major differences in procedure where breakup of a relationship is involved are that Domestic Violence Act cases are started by an Application, rather than by a Particulars of Claim, and that divorce proceedings are started by petition. Legal aid and advice is available for contested divorces and for applications under the Domestic Violence Act: see Appendix 2. However, legal aid is not available for uncontested divorce proceedings, although legal advice can be sought for assistance in filling in the forms and advice on what to do.

(iii) *Rehousing*

A woman who leaves the domestic home because of violence or the fear of violence is considered to be homeless for the purposes of the Housing (Homeless Persons) Act 1977: see Chapter 10. Local authorities have in the past shown some reluctance to respond swiftly and efficiently to the demands of women who have left the domestic home, for fear of allegations that by easing the housing situation for them, they are actively contributing to the breakup of a family unit. As a result of the Domestic Violence Act and the Housing (Homeless Persons) Act, this attitude should now disappear, although where it is still encountered, authorities should be reminded that it is no part of their duties to use their housing strength and the fear of homelessness as a way of forcing a woman back to an unhappy homelife.

Authorities sometimes are slow to respond to demands for rehousing because their experience shows them that frequently, perhaps more often than not, a woman who has left her husband or partner will return after a short while. This itself may be a reflection of the attitude described in the last paragraph, and general social pressures. They fear disruption of their housing allocation programmes. They should be reminded that in a sufficient number of cases to justify any such disruption, a breakup is final and that, in any event, it is no part of their business to add to the pressures that a woman who has just left her home will be under. Rather, they should use their housing powers to alleviate her stress.

A woman who is not rehoused by the local authority will have difficulties finding anywhere else to live. She should bear in mind the provisions of the Sex Discrimination Act which make it unlawful for anyone concerned in the management, sale or rental of property to treat a woman any the less favourably than he would treat a man, for example, by refusing to grant a mortgage to a woman, or adding some term such as a demand for a guarantor for rent or mortgage payments. This Act does not apply to resident landlords or buildings so small that they are either subdivided into no more than three separate units of accommodation or can only accommodate a maximum of six people within them. A housing association set up to cater for the needs of one sex only, *e.g.* single mothers, female ex-prisoners, male ex-mental patients, etc., is also exempt from the Act. Unlawful discrimination can be the subject of a normal county court action.

Further Reading

Undefended Divorces, free from the Divorce Registry, Somerset House, Strand, London, WC2;

Coote, A. and Gill, T., *Women's Rights, A Practical Guide* (Penguin).
Coote, A. and Gill, T., *Battered Women and the New Law*, Inter-Action & N.C.C.L.
Faulder, C., Jackson, C. and Lewis, M., *The Women's Directory*, (Virago).
"Obtaining Injunctions for Battered Women," August 1977 LAG Bulletin 185.

10 Homelessness

Like domestic violence, the law relating to homelessness has been the subject of recent legislation: the housing (Homeless Persons) Act 1977. Both Acts were the result of considerable campaign pressure over a number of years. In the case of homelessness, books like *Homelessness in London* by Greve and others and *Homeless Near A Thousand Homes* by Bryan Glastonbury, the work of Shelter, the National Campaign for the Homeless, and even a memorable television programme (*Cathy Come Home*), contributed to the growth in public awareness of the depth and extent of the problem. There are many who consider that bad housing conditions are responsible not only for homelessness, but also as a factor leading to domestic violence.

The state of the law in relation to homelessness before the Act came into force on December 1, 1977 was very unsettled. Under the National Assistance Act 1948, local authorities, through their social services departments, were under a duty to provide temporary accommodation, but only for those who had become unforseeably homeless. In 1974, the Local Government Act 1972 reduced this duty to a mere power, although the duty was subsequently reimposed by ministerial circular. At the same time, the Department of the Environment sought to shift responsibility for the homeless from the social service authorities, to housing authorities. This move constituted a recognition that homelessness was not so much a matter of individual responsibility but part of the overall deficiency in the housing situation. In the event, while some local authorities co-operated with this change, others did not. This led to a highly unsatisfactory situation, for in some areas, housing and social services are the responsibilities of different local authorities.

In practice, what this meant was that the homeless were

being shuttled back and forth between different authorities: sometimes, for the reasons referred to in the last paragraph, within one area; at other times because local authorities formed the view that the responsibility lay not with themselves but with a local authority for another area, *e.g.* where the person in question last lived. Another cause of dissatisfaction was the High Court decision in *Roberts* v. *Dorset County Council*, which held that the duty was, indeed, only a duty to provide *temporary* accommodation and that the local authority in question in that case had not behaved wrongly when they decided to terminate the provision of bed and breakfast accommodation to a family with one child who had nowhere else to go.

Towards these difficulties, the 1977 Act is directed. It provides the first-ever statutory definition of homelessness. It places responsibility squarely on housing, rather than social services authorities. It defines when one local authority can avoid its duties by reason of "local connection" with the area of another. And it also obliges local authorities to provide full and permanent rehousing to those who qualify under the Act. At the same time, the Act does not place this duty on authorities in respect of everyone who is homeless. To be entitled in law to the full duty of permanent rehousing, a person must be homeless, must not have become homeless intentionally, and must have a priority need. There are lesser duties towards those who, as it were, fall foul of one of the qualifying conditions or another.

The result is a fairly complex piece of legislation. Nonetheless, it is legislation with which a social worker must be wholly familiar: when an individual or a family is homeless, or threatened with homelessness, he will be more reliant than at other times upon support from others. There is plenty of scope for the social worker to use his knowledge and to assist the homeless person through the maze of official enquiries which will be the immediate result of an application for rehousing under the 1977 Act.

In outline, the procedure will be as follows:

A person who is homeless or threatened with homelessness applies to the correct local authority office for rehousing under the Act. From that time on, the local authority is under some degree of duty towards him. The duty will not, however, amount to a full duty of permanent rehousing until such time as the authority has completed all its enquiries. These enquiries are directed towards the qualifying conditions and if at any stage the authority forms the view that the duty which they owe to the individual in question is *not* that full duty of permanent rehousing, it is obliged to give reasons for its decision, in writing. During this period, there may also be duties to provide temporary accommodation.

Under s. 12 of the Act, a local authority affected by it is bound to "have regard to" the *Code of Guidance* which has been issued by the Department of the Environment. The *Code* does not have the force of law, but it is a highly influential document. Any authority which completely disregarded or ignored it would be acting in breach of the law and its decisions could be impeached in the Divisional Court: see Appendix 1. But being obliged to have regard to a document is not the same as being obliged to comply with it. A local authority can deviate from the guidance contained in the *Code*, although it ought to have a good reason for doing so. Paragraph references (*e.g.* 1.1., or A1.1.) in the text are to paragraphs of the *Code*.

The easiest way to approach the Act is by way of a checklist. The actual meaning of each phrase used is described below, under separate headings, and it is important to follow with some care the exact words used.

(i) Individual makes application for rehousing under the Act.

Q. Is there reason to believe that he is homeless or threatened with homelessness?

A. Yes, simply because an application has been made, and until the authority forms a contrary view.

Duty: to make further enquiries.

(ii) Authority makes enquiries.

Q. Is the applicant homeless or threatened with homelessness?

A. No.

Duty: to give reasons for decision.

or

A. Yes.

Duty: to make further enquiries.

(iii) Authority continues enquiries.

Q. Does the applicant have a priority need for accommodation?

A. No.

Duty: to give appropriate advice and assistance, and to give reasons for decision.

or

A. Yes.

Duty: to continue enquiries, *and ask*

Q. Is the applicant already homeless?

A. No.

Duty: no further duties until applicant becomes homeless.

or

A. Yes.

Duty: to provide temporary accommodation pending completion of enquiries. This also applies even if the authority only has reason to believe that the applicant has a priority need, *i.e.* has not yet formed a final view on this question.

(iv) Authority continues enquiries.

Q. Did the applicant become homeless or threatened with homelessness intentionally?

A. No.

Duty: subject to (v), below, to provide rehousing for an applicant who is already homeless, and to ensure that accommodation does not cease to be available to a person who is merely threatened with homelessness. In effect, this means to provide him with rehousing once he actually becomes homeless.

or

A. Yes.

Duty: to give reasons for decision, appropriate advice and assistance, *and ask*

Q. Is the applicant already homeless?

A. No.

Duty: no further duties until applicant becomes homeless.

or

A. Yes.

Duty: to provide temporary accommodation for such period as the authority considers will give him a reasonable opportunity of himself securing his own accommodation.

(v) Authority *may* make further enquiries.

Q. Does the applicant or anyone who might reasonably be expected to live with him have a local connection with its area?

A. Yes.

Duty: as under (iv), above.

or

A. No.

Q. Does the applicant or anyone who might reasonably be expected to live with him have a local connection with the area of another authority?

A. No.

Duty: as under (iv), above.

or

A. Yes.

Duty: to consider next question.

Q. Will either the applicant or anyone who might reasonably be expected to live with him run the risk of domestic violence in that other area?

A. Yes.

Duty: as under (iv), above.

or

A. No.

Duty: to notify applicant of reasons for decision, to notify other authority of its view, to provide temporary accommodation until completion of enquiries by other authority. If other authority accepts duty, it is under full rehousing duty. In the event of dispute between authorities, there is an arbitration procedure devised by the Department of the Environment.

The rest of this chapter will be concerned with the following questions:

1. Which authorities are affected by the Act?
2. What is homelessness?
3. Who has a priority need for accommodation?
4. Who has become homeless or threatened with homelessness intentionally?
5. Which authority is responsible under the Act?
6. How are decisions notified?
7. What sort of accommodation must be provided?
8. What other provisions there are in the Act?
9. What alternative possibilities are there?

1. *Housing Authorities*

The Act affects housing authorities only. In London, this means London Borough Councils, rather than the Greater London Council. In non-metropolitan authority areas, housing is the responsibility of the district council, while social services is that of the county council. In metropolitan authority areas, both social services and housing are the responsibilities of the district councils.

2. *Homelessness*

The Act is only concerned with people who are homeless or threatened with homelessness: see (i), above. Applicants should bear in mind the criminal provisions described in 8, below, which deal with people who make false statements in order to try and get rehousing under the Act. Once an application is made, then authorities will have reason to believe that a person is homeless or threatened with homelessness, until its enquiries compel them to form a contrary view. The *Code* (2.2.) lists a number of matters which enquiries will normally cover. Authorities are urged (2.3.) to be both quick and sympathetic and to recognise (2.4.) that those in need of help may be under strain, may be confused and may have difficulty explaining their position clearly and logically. Authorities are asked to be ready to agree to someone else being present during interviews, such as a friend of the applicant, or some other person whom the applicant knows and trusts, *e.g.* a social worker.

The Act defines "threatened with homelessness" in relation to the definition of homelessness itself. A person is threatened with homelessness if it is likely that he will become homeless within 28 days of the application for assistance. This period of 28 days has been selected because most possession orders only take effect after 28 days. The *Code* (2.1.) urges authorities to offer assistance at the earliest possible time, so as to avoid any unnecessary additional distress.

A person is homeless (s. 1) if he has no accommodation available for occupation by himself *together with* any member of his family who is living with him *and* any other person who normally lives with him in circumstances in which the housing authority considers it reasonable for that person to do so. "Member of family" is not confined to legal or blood relatives: it applies to people who are cohabiting and, *e.g.* foster children. The *Code* gives as an example of "persons who normally reside with (the applicant) in circumstances in which the housing authority considers it reasonable for that person to reside with him" the elderly or disabled person who has a housekeeper or companion to live with him. There is caselaw in which a cohabitee of long-standing is considered to be a member of the family (*Dyson Holdings* v. *Fox*) and the *Code* also adopts this view.

The policy of the Act, as emphasised in the *Code* (4.2.) is to try and keep families together. Under the earlier provisions, it was quite common for children to be taken into care for no other reason than that the family had become homeless. This was often followed by a refusal to consider the family for rehousing, on the grounds that there were no children living with the family. An alternative Catch-22 was to offer the parents accommodation that was not big enough for the children — because the children were in care — and because there would then not be sufficient accommodation for them, the children would be kept indefinitely in care:

> "The practice of splitting families is not acceptable, even for short periods. The social cost, personal hardship and long term damage to children, as well as the expense involved in receiving children into care, rules this out as an acceptable course, other than in the exceptional case where professional social work advice is that there are compelling reasons, apart from homelessness, for separating a child from his family."

Accommodation is only available to a person and his family, as defined above, if there is somewhere

(a) which he is entitled to occupy because he has an interest in it, i.e. ownership or tenancy; or

(b) which he is entitled to occupy because there is a court order permitting him to do so, *e.g.* in matrimonial proceedings, see Chapter 9; or

(c) which he is entitled to occupy because he has a contractual or bare licence to live there; or

(d) which he is entitled to occupy because it would be illegal to evict him (see Chapter 8.) This covers, *e.g.* a former unprotected tenant who is entitled to remain in occupation of the premises until a landlord has obtained a possession order against him.

A person is also homeless if he normally lives, with his family as defined above, in a caravan or houseboat and there is nowhere for them both to park/moor it *and* live in it. In addition, even though a person would appear to have accommodation available within one of the four sets of circumstances described above, a person is also homeless if

(a) he has been locked out of the premises in question, *e.g.* because of an illegal eviction; *or*

(b) occupation of the premises would lead to violence from some other person living in them, *or* would lead to threats of violence from some other person living in the premises and that other person is likely to carry those threats out. This provision is designed to deal principally with battered women. The *Code* asks authorities to treat applications from women who are in fear of violence sympathetically, and reminds authorities that the mere fact that violence has not yet occurred does not mean that it is not likely to do so (2.10.).

3. *Priority Need*

If an authority decides that a person is homeless or threatened with homelessness but does *not* have a priority need, then it is under a duty to provide appropriate advice and assistance to the applicant. The *Code* (6.1.-6.5.) suggests that authorities could advise on the possibilities of the rent and rates rebate/allowance scheme, see Chapter 7, or on the possibility of registration of a fair rent, see Chapter 4. It could also advise on what help might be available from a housing aid centre, and could keep lists of lodgings, hostels, housing associations, etc. If there is a priority need, then the position is as described in (iii), above.

A person has a priority need for accommodation under the Act (s. 2) if:

(a) He has dependent children living with him, or who might reasonably be expected to live with him; *or*

(b) He became homeless or threatened with homelessness as a result of any emergency such as flood, fire or any other disaster; *or*

(c) He, or anyone who either does or might reasonably be expected to live with him, is vulnerable because of old age, mental illness, physical disability or other special reason; *or*

(d) She, or, if a man, a woman who either does or who might reasonably be expected to live with him, is pregnant, no matter how long- or short-lived the pregnancy.

The *Code* (2.12.) describes all children under the age of 16 as dependent, as well as children under the age of 19 who are receiving full-time education or training, and those other children who cannot support themselves independently. The children need not be the children of the applicant. They could be, for example, grandchildren, adopted or foster-children. The priority need will be established even if the children have been sent to stay with friends of family because of the homelessness as they will still be children who might reasonably be expected to live with the applicant.

Those over normal retirement age, 65 for men, 60 for women, are to be treated as vulnerable because of old age, and so should those who, although they are only approaching retirement age, are particularly frail or in poor health. Authorities are asked to take a generous view of "disability," and to draw on the assistance of area health and social service authorities in reaching their decisions. As examples of "other special reason," the *Code* mentions battered women without children who are at risk of violent pursuit, or who are likely to be at risk of further violence if they return home, and homeless young children who are at risk of sexual and financial exploitation.

4. *Intentional Homelessness*

A person who is homeless or threatened with homelessness and has a priority need, but who became homeless or threatened with homelessness intentionally will be entitled to appropriate advice and assistance, as described above. In addition, if the applicant is already actually homeless, he is entitled to accommodation for such period as the authority considers will give him a reasonable opportunity to find his own alternative accommodation (s. 4(3)): see 9, below. Especially where children are involved, authorities should not be too quick to withdraw accommodation and they should provide sufficient help to make sure that the family is not left without any shelter at all (4.1.) Note that it is up to the authority to satisfy itself that a person did become homeless or threatened with homelessness intentionally, not up to the applicant to prove that he did not. If the applicant did *not* become homeless or threatened with homelessness intentionally, then the position is as described in (iv), above.

Intentional homelessness is defined in s. 17 of the Act:

"A person becomes homeless intentionally if he deliberately does or fails to do anything in consequence of which he ceases to occupy accommodation which is available for his occupation and which it would have been reasonable for him to continue to occupy."

"A person becomes threatened with homelessness intentionally if he deliberately does or fails to do anything the likely result of which is that he will be forced to leave accommodation which is available for his occupation and which it would have been reasonable for him to continue to occupy."

There is some alleviation of this rather rigid formula:

"An act or omission in good faith on the part of a person who was unaware of any relevant fact is not to be treated as deliberate." This includes people who fall into rent or mortgage arrears, unaware of the right to register a rent (Chapter 4) or receive assistance by way of rebate or allowance (Chapter 7), or those who simply left accommodation on receipt of notice to do so, unaware of the right to remain (2.17.)

In addition, "regard may be had, in determining ... whether it would have been reasonable for a person to continue to occupy accommodation, to the general circumstances prevailing in relation to housing in the area of the housing authority to whom he applied for accommodation or for assistance ... " This is a difficult criterion to apply. Occupiers themselves are rarely aware of the general problems of an area, for example, that there are many others who are also being harassed, or who lack basic amenities, or who live in appalling conditions. But comparison with others is what the *Code* (2.16.) suggests that the authority should engage in when determining whether the applicant has acted reasonably or not.

Someone who chooses to sell his home, or who has been evicted because of persistent and wilful refusal to pay rent will normally be regarded as having done or failed to do something resulting in intentional homelessness (2.15.) But someone who lost a home because of mortgage or rent arrears which were the result of genuine financial difficulties should not be considered intentionally homeless, or threatened with homelessness, nor will a person who quite simply cannot manage his own affairs properly. It is not intentional homelessness for a woman to leave home because of violence, or as a result of becoming pregnant, for example, because of subsequent parental difficulties (2.16.) People who leave accommodation which is unsatisfactory, for example, because of overcrowding, lack of basic amenities, condition of the property, perhaps serious harassment, will not normally be considered to have become intentionally homeless unless the incidence of these throughout the area in question is so severe that, despite the conditions, it would have been reasonable to go on putting up with them.

A person is only intentionally homeless or threatened with homelessness if he could, in any event, have gone on occupying the last accommodation. To know whether this is the case or not, a knowledge of housing law will often be necessary. The *Code* (A1.2.) suggests that housing authority officials may need a working knowledge of the Rent Act and it may be that the social worker will find the most common use for the knowledge acquired from the earlier chapters of this book in this connection.

One fear which many have had is that authorities will refuse to rehouse people who have not waited until a court order is made against them. On a strict interpretation of s. 17, any former tenant, whether or not protected, could be described as having become intentionally homeless if he left the property before an order was made. It would, of course, be illegal for the landlord to evict without a court order and until the order is made, the occupier could qualify as having accommodation available under 2, above.

This could lead to unnecessary expense and, possibly, the distress of pointless court proceedings, where there could be no defence to the action, for example, because there is a resident landlord, or one of the grounds for possession is clearly capable of being established as a result of which the court will have to make an order, *e.g.* returning owner-occupier or retirement home.

The *Code* (A1.3.) suggests that it will not always be appropriate for authorities to insist on a court order. In an appropriate case, the authority should accept a letter from, for example, a landlord's solicitor, setting out the position. In many cases, however, this will not be possible. For example, where the ground for possession is one of those where the court has a discretion whether or not to make the order, for example, rent arrears, nuisance and annoyance, greater hardship, and might only grant an order suspended indefinitely, then it will normally be necessary to retain possession until a court makes an order for possession. It may also be a form of intentional homelessness for an occupier within the jurisdiction of the Rent Tribunal not to apply for suspension of notice, provided he knew of his right to do so.

It is the most immediate cause of homelessness which must be considered (2.18.) For example, a person who leaves one home, even a secure home, to move in with relatives or friends, who subsequently find that they cannot put him up, would not be considered intentionally homeless. Those who are deprived of their rights because an authority comes to a view that they have become intentionally homeless will not lose their rights to rehousing indefinitely. For example, a family might become intentionally homeless and be refused rehousing. They might then succeed in obtaining a tenancy from a resident landlord. The tenant may apply for registration of rent. The landlord then may not permit the tenant to remain in occupation any longer than he is bound to do so: see Chapter 5. At that point, there will be no defence to possession proceedings and the tenant could not be considered intentionally homeless. Indeed, the authority should not even insist that he remains in occupation until an order is made.

5. *Local Connection*

An authority is not obliged to enquire into the question of local
connection, and in many cases it will quite obviously be a
pointless exercise to do so. The provisions (s. 5) have been
designed to avert the former practice of quibbling between
authorities as to with which the homeless person had the
greater local connection. As the law now stands, an application must be accepted unless the applicant and anyone who
might reasonably be expected to live with him has *no* connection with the area to which he applies, and *does* have a
connection with another, subject to the overriding provision
relating to domestic violence:

(a) Neither the applicant nor anyone who might reasonably
be expected to live with him has a local connection with the
area to which the application is made; *and*

(b) the applicant or a person who might reasonably be
expected to live with him does have a local connection with the
area of another authority; *and*

(c) neither the applicant nor anyone who might reasonably
be expected to live with him runs the risk of domestic violence
in the other area.

Unless all of these qualifications apply, the provisions have
no relevance at all and if the other conditions, described
above, are fulfilled, the first authority must rehouse. Local
connection is itself defined in s. 18 as

(a) an area in which a person is or in the past was normally
resident of his own choice; or

(b) an area in which he is employed; or

(c) an area with which the applicant has family association;
or

(d) an area with which for some other special reason the
applicant has a connection.

The term "resident of choice" is one which excludes residence while in the armed forces, and residence while detained
in prison or a mental hospital. Similarly, a person is not
employed in another area if the employment is in the armed
forces. If there is more than one other area with which the
applicant may have a local connection, then in deciding where
first to try and shift the responsibility, the first authority

should take into account the applicant's own wishes (5.3.)

Once an authority to which an application has been made forms the view that the local connection provisions apply, it will notify the other authority in question. It will also notify the applicant of its decision. The second authority must then form its own view on exactly the same issues and if it reaches the same decision, will take over responsibility for the applicant. If it does not, the matter may be referred to arbitration. Until a decision is made, the first authority must provide accommodation for the applicant and his family, as defined.

6. *Notification*

An authority to which an application is made is obliged to give decisions, in writing, with reasons, whenever it forms a view that means, in practice, that it is not under a full duty of permanent rehousing. Because, in many cases, the applicant will have nowhere to receive correspondence, such decisions must be kept available for collection at the office of the housing department in question for a reasonable period after the decision has been made. Most authorities have already printed out pro-forma decisions, for example, listing all the conditions for priority need. This is not the most helpful approach as it gives no clue at all as to the basis upon which a view of the facts has been reached, in those cases where the authority and the applicant are in dispute as to, for example, whether or not he became intentionally homeless, whether or not he has dependent children who might reasonably be expected to live with him. Because the Act is so new, no case has yet come before the courts in which the extent of reasoning which an authority must supply has been defined.

7. *Accommodation*

Regardless of whether or not accommodation provided under the Act is for permanent use or only temporary use, it must be up to the standards contained in general housing and public health legislation (4.3.): see, *Housing: Repairs and Improvements*.

The full rehousing duty means that an authority must secure

the provision of accommodation to someone who is already homeless, and must secure that accommodation does not cease to be available to someone who is threatened with homelessness, *i.e.* by having something ready for immediate occupation when he eventually has to leave the existing accommodation. Accommodation in all cases must be such as will be sufficient not only for the applicant, but also for anyone who might reasonably be expected to reside with him (s. 16.) The *Code* suggests (4.4.) that it should normally consist of self-contained accommodation *i.e.* not bed and breakfast. The authority can charge for accommodation (s. 10).

The authority does not have to provide the accommodation itself. It could arrange for rehousing by, *e.g.* a housing association, or even a private landlord. These remarks apply whether the duty to rehouse is a full duty, or where it is a temporary duty, for example, where the applicant is homeless, has a priority need but became homeless intentionally, or pending the outcome of some decision.

8. *Other Provisions*

In connection with the duties described above, a local authority has power to take steps to protect the property of someone who has applied to them. In some cases, there is a positive duty (s. 7) to do so where there is a danger of loss or damage to property because of the applicant's inability to protect or deal with it himself. This duty arises if accommodation is being provided pending the outcome of enquiries, or for a period to permit someone who became intentionally homeless but who has a priority need to find somewhere else to live, or to provide accommodation pending a decision over local connection, or where the full rehousing duty exists. It also arises when the authority is under a duty to ensure that accommodation does not cease to be available to a person who is threatened with homelessness and has a priority need.

In other cases, even where the authority is not obliged to take such steps to protect property, it has power to do so. In relation to both power and duty, the authority has powers of entry into premises to deal with an applicant's property. Once it takes property into storage, as it will normally do, it can charge for the storage and it cannot bring an end to the storage arrangement without notification to the applicant of its decision to do so, and the reasons for it.

In addition to these powers, there are provisions to deal with applicants who make false statements to the authority in order to get rehousing under the Act. A person commits an offence if he, with the intention of making an authority believe that a person who has applied for rehousing under the Act is either homeless or threatened with homelessness or has a priority need, or did not become homeless or threatened with homelessness intentionally,

(a) knowingly or recklessly lies in a material particular to the authority; or

(b) withholds information reasonably required by the authority in connection with an application.

It is also an offence for an applicant to fail to notify an authority of any change of facts material to the application which occur before the applicant receives notification of the decision on the application. The authority, however, has to explain the duty to inform of material change in clear and ordinary language, and must also explain the possibility of criminal penalties. It is a defence to this charge to show that the warning was not given, or that although it was given, the applicant has a good excuse for failing to conform. It may be a good excuse that the applicant did not understand the caution.

9. *Alternative Possibilities*

As must be clear from the foregoing, there will be many who will not be entitled to compel a local authority to rehouse them. This does not mean that a local authority will not provide rehousing. Some authorities house more people than they are obliged to do under the Act. It is always worthwhile asking to be put on the housing waiting list, even if excluded from the benefit of the Act.

Housing associations may be a good further source of rehousing. Some of them cater for specific classes of people. Although, of course, it is hard to get accommodation in the private sector, it may not be impossible, particularly if there is a resident landlord. This may provide a sufficient period of new housing to justify a new claim under the Act when it later comes to an end through no fault of the occupier. It may, in a few cases, be worthwhile considering the possibility of mortgage.

There are some agencies which will provide short-life accommodation for the homeless, *i.e.* in property which is to be demolished or redeveloped. Where the alternative is hostel or bed-and-breakfast accommodation, most people express a preference for short-life property as, at least, some semblance of normal family life can be continued. The use of short-life property for these purposes, as an immediate solution to the problem of homelessness is advocated by Ron Bailey in his book *The Homeless and the Empty Houses*. However, there are dangers in this course:

Most people hate short-life once they get into it. They cannot do major repair works, because it is too expensive and not financially viable in view of the likely life of the property, even if the occupier could afford it. Most such properties are in such a dilapidated condition that minor repairs and redecoration will not be of much use. But once a person has short-life accommodation, *e.g.* for 9 months or a year, it may be impossible to get him rehousing for the whole of that period as he will not be homeless for the purposes of the Act. In some cases, it *may* be wiser to put up with a shorter period in a hostel or bed-and-breakfast if this will induce the local authority to grant permanent rehousing quickly.

Further Reading

The Housing (Homeless Persons) Act 1977, Martin Partington, Sweet & Maxwell;

"The Housing (Homeless Persons) Act 1977, November 1977 LAG Bulletin 259.

"A Guide to the Housing (Homeless Persons) Act 1977, CHAS/CHAR/ CPAG/National Council for One-Parent Families/National Women's Aid Federation/SHAC/Shelter.

Appendix 1: Legal Proceedings

The general course of any civil legal proceeding is as follows:

(i) *Summons/Writ*

This first stage refers to the formal issue of proceedings.

(ii) *Particulars/Statement of Claim*

These are the facts which support the Plaintiff's case and set out the remedy which is sought.

(iii) *Defence*

This is the defendant's answer.

(iv) *Further Pleadings*

These may include (a) a counterclaim by the defendant which is in all respects like a Particulars/Statement of Claim, save that the defendant does not have to issue it separately but can make the claim in the course of the same proceedings, provided the claim arises out of the same or relevant matters; (b) a Defence to Counterclaim, which is the plaintiff's answer to the counterclaim; (c) Request for Further and Better Particulars by one side or the other, asking for further or more closely particularised details about Particulars/Statement of Claim, Defence and/or Counterclaim, etc; (d) Further and Better Particulars, which is the answer to the request; (e) in some cases, a Plaintiff may wish to place on the record a formal Reply to the Defence, or a Defendant might Reply to the Defence to Counterclaim. In addition to all of these documents which seek either to elaborate upon or elicit further information about the matter before the court, there may be a process known as (f) Discovery of Documents, in which each side must declare what documents, if any, he has or has had in his possession which are relevant to the case. These are listed in sections of (A) those which the other party is entitled to see and which may be inspected on demand, (B) those which the party making the declaration no longer has custody or control over, and (C) those which the party making the declaration has but will not permit the other side to see because they are "privileged," *i.e.* they are documents which are part of the materials being used for the preparation of the case, *e.g.* correspondence between lawyer and client or witness, witness' statements, instructions to a barrister to present the case in court.

(v) *Pre-Trial Review/Summons for Directions*

This is a short hearing designed to sort out the state of the pleadings. It may take place before any documents other than the Particulars/Statement of Claim have been served, or at any stage during the exchange of pleadings, and orders will be made requiring the service of such further pleadings as are considered appropriate within specified time limits. In addition, questions about the trial will be discussed, for example, how long it will take, and one side or the other might seek the directions as to matters touching the trial, e.g. the number of expert witnesses who may be called.

(vi) *Trial*

There may be several, successive dates listed for a trial, which may be adjourned, for example, because one side or the other is not ready and either the opponent agrees to an adjournment or the court accepts that there ought to be one and orders a new, later date, or because there is not enough time in the court to hear the matter; the trial has several, formal stages:

(a) Plaintiff (but usually his representative) opens case with speech outlining the issues the judge will have to decide;

(b) Plaintiff calls witnesses, each of whom will be taken through his evidence by the Plaintiff's representative; each will normally be cross-examined by the Defendant's representative;

(c) Defendant calls witnesses, and the same process will be repeated, only in reverse;

(d) Defendant's representative closes case with speech to Judge remarking on the evidence, if necessary, and addressing him on the law;

(e) Plaintiff's representative's answer to closing speech for the defence;

(f) Judgment in which judge sums up evidence, states what facts he finds to be true, deals with appropriate law and decides who wins, or who wins what issues;

(g) Order in which judge grants remedies to parties as appropriate and deals with questions of costs;

(vii) *Execution*

Possibly after a delay ordered by the judge, a warrant will be issued, in possession cases entitling the bailiffs to evict the occupier.

This is a simple outline only, designed to permit the reader to follow the various stages of procedure which can frequently mystify the lay observer or participant and often appear irrational. In theory, the pre-trial stages are designed to set before the judge as much as possible that can be agreed between the parties, for example, facts which they agree to be true, and which serve to identify just what it is that the judge is being called upon to decide, *i.e.* what the issues between the parties are. Cases will frequently be conducted with greater simplicity, especially when parties are not represented by lawyers. In such cases, the Particulars/Statement of Claim may be highly informal, or else on a proforma provided by the court. Particulars of Claim and Summons are terms which apply to the early stages in the county courts; Statement of Claim and Writ apply to the High Court.

We shall now look at some of these matters in slightly closer detail, concentrating on those which are most likely to be relevant to a housing case:

1. *The County Court*

It is in the county court that most matters concerning housing rights will be heard. There is a county court for every part of the country. The county court can normally only deal with matters where the value of what is claimed does not exceed £2000. It is, therefore, normally necessary for there to be a claim for a sum of money up to this amount before the county court has jurisdiction to exercise any of its powers. However, in addition, the county court has power to grant possession orders where the rateable value of the premises in question does not exceed Rent Act limits, *i.e.* £1500 in Greater London and £750 elsewhere; it has the power to grant injunctions even though there is no monetary claim at all in the circumstances described in Chapters 8 and 9, *i.e.* harassment, illegal eviction and domestic violence; and it has power to make a declaration as to what the legal position of the parties is where what is involved in a question under the Rent Act.

The remedies most commonly sought in the county court will be:

(i) Possession of premises, by a landlord, who may also seek

(ii) Damages for injury to the premises caused by the occupier. An occupier might also be seeking damages from a landlord, for disrepair, or for loss or suffering related to harassment or illegal eviction, in which case he is likely also to want

(iii) An injunction, compelling the landlord to do something. If either party is disputing the true nature of the arrangement or the extent to which the Rent Act protects the letting, then either may seek, alone or in conjunction with any of the remedies mentioned above

(iv) A Declaration, as to the correct legal position.

In addition, a landlord will normally be claiming arrears of rent and/or a sum by way of damages for use and occupation which is known as (v) mesne (pronounced "mean") profits. Whoever wins will be wanting the other side to pay his (vi) costs. If the court orders the occupier to give up possession of the premises, the landlord will seek a (vii) warrant for possession and may also seek to (viii) execute a monetary judgment. Similarly, if an occupier has been awarded damages against his landlord, he will want to execute the monetary judgment, if the landlord does not pay up voluntarily. An occupier may also have difficulty forcing the landlord to obey an injunction, in which case his only recourse is to re-apply to the court for the landlord to suffer (ix) committal for contempt.

(i) *Possession*

The Particulars of Claim attached to the summons will indicate the grounds on which the landlord is alleging that he is entitled to recover possession. This may mean Rent Act grounds (see Chapter 4) or it may mean that the landlord is alleging that the occupier is no more than a licensee (see Chapter 2) or that the tenancy is not protected at all (see Chapters 5 and 6.) Similarly, possession might be sought by a mortgage company against an owner-occupier (see Chapter 3.) When possession is sought from a tenant or former tenant, the summons itself must not be issued until the notice to quit has run out. If possession is sought against a licensee or former licensee, it is enough to show that the license has come to an end before the proceedings are heard, *i.e.* the trial, unless the speedy procedures, Order 26 in the county court, Order 113 in the High Court, are being used, in which case the licence must have expired by the date the application was issued.

Orders 26 and 113 differ from the course of normal proceedings in that they are designed to be quicker, cheaper and simpler. They can be heard extremely quickly and there is not normally anything like the full extent of pre-trial procedure. Shortly, a landlord states his case, not in a Particulars/Statement of Claim but in an Application and if the occupier has any defence, he simply files an affidavit (sworn statement).

Many occupiers find receipt of a court document extremely intimidating. Some even think that the summons or application constitutes the formal order itself. A summons for possession will have a form attached to it, which invites the occupier to state if there is a defence to the claim, or if he wishes to admit the landlord's right to claim possession back. This form should not be completed and returned unless the occupier, and his advisers, are completely sure that there is no defence, especially bearing in mind the provisions of the Housing (Homeless Persons) Act 1977, see Chapter 10, or what the defence is. If advice is needed, this may be obtained in one of the ways suggested in Appendix 2.

The summons will declare that the occupier must return the form of admission or defence within 14 days. Although it is best not to be dilatory, it does not matter if it is filed later, so long as it is filed before the date listed for the trial. This date will appear on the summons. Normally, if a case is to be contested, it will be adjourned. Occupiers who are unrepresented are often considered to be at a disadvantage in court so full use of the legal aid system (Appendix 2) should be encouraged. Even if a case is to be adjourned, it is still necessary to attend on the day stated, unless the court notifies otherwise.

(ii) *Damages*

Landlords frequently add a claim for damages, for example, to the premises, as a way of further intimidating an occupier. In fact, many possession actions are settled and the claim is not pursued although, again, one must be wary of jeopardising the occupier's position as regards rehousing, *i.e.* insofar as it may be impeded by intentional homelessness: see Chapter 10. Courts, which are often sympathetic to landlords' claims for possession, tend to take a fairly realistic view of claims for damages, often now being aware of what sort of conditions are to be found in the private rented sector and also appreciating that the landlord has, in regaining vacant possession, already acquired a valuable asset. The position as regards mesne profits (see (v) below) is different.

When an occupier seeks damages, for example, for disrepair to premises, courts also tend to put low values on their claims. Such a claim may be attached to an application for an injunction (see (iii) below), either or both of which may be claimed during an action initiated by the occupier, or may be claimed by way of counterclaim. It is not permissible to withhold rent because of disrepair, but if premises are in bad condition and the landlord seeks possession on the ground of arrears of rent, then it may well be that a claim for damages by the occupier will result in the landlord owing him money, despite or even allowing for the arrears. What might be claimed by way of damages for harassment or illegal eviction has been suggested in Chapter 8. In all cases, whoever is claiming damages, the total must not exceed £2000.

(iii) *An Injunction*

This will often be the true remedy that an occupier seeks in cases of harassment or illegal eviction, or, indeed, disrepair (see *Housing: Repairs and Improvements.*) In the first two cases, it is not necessary to attach a claim for damages, but there will usually be one. Strictly, a court is reluctant to issue a mandatory injunction, *i.e.* one which tells the landlord to *do* something, as opposed to an injunction restraining him from doing something. This is, however, in almost every case a matter of phraseology: for example, restraining the landlord from interfering with the tenant's quiet enjoyment of premises by depriving him of the supply of gas and electricity to them, or access to them, in place of ordering the landlord to restore gas and electricity to the premises, or to readmit the tenant.

When an injunction is sought before the end of the case, it will be necessary to file an affidavit in support of the application. An affidavit is sworn before a solicitor, commissioner for oaths or an officer of the court appointed to the task. The idea is that in interim hearings, there should not be oral evidence, examination and cross-examination, but that the judge should decide the relevant question of balance of convenience on the facts as set out in the affidavits. It is also necessary to issue special applications for such hearings, i.e. in addition to the summons for the main trial of the action.

(iv) *A Declaration*

This is commonly sought when either Rent Officer or Rent Tribunal is refusing jurisdiction, or else, without that element, because the parties want to clear up the legal issues before the practical questions of rent control and security actually arise, *e.g.* during "fixed term" agreement. Unless a declaration is sought in conjunction with some other remedy, although there may be an order for the costs of the action (see (vi) below), there will be no other order and no one will have to do or refrain from doing anything as a result of it. Its principal value is that a later date, for example, if the occupier does not leave and the landlord starts possession proceedings, the issue is decided between them and cannot be re-opened. Otherwise than when an appeal is involved, once a court has decided an issue between two people, the matter cannot be argued between them all over again on a separate occasion. This is only so, however, provided the issue is dealing with exactly the same facts, e.g. not a new instance of harassment, disrepair, nuisance, arrears, etc.

(v) *Mesne profits*

Mesne profits are damages for use and occupation of premises, otherwise than under a contractual agreement, whether tenancy or licence. A landlord can claim mesne profits for what he has lost or suffered by reason of the occupation, up to the time the court orders the occupier to leave. When the occupier is a former tenant or licensee, the amount of mesne profits will normally equal the same sum that has been paid by way of rent during the agreement. If a landlord wants to claim more, alleging some special loss because of the occupier's failure to leave when the agreement came to an end, *e.g.* failure to complete a sale, he should specify this in detail, explaining how the amount has been calculated. The court will not normally grant more than the same that was paid in rent, although it has power to do so, and an extra amount is rarely claimed not least of all because it is rare that a landlord is able to recover the sum of money involved. Quite apart from the difficulty and expense of tracing a former occupier, who may now be homeless, he is in any event unlikely to have much if any money at all.

Mesne profits may pose more of a problem where there is no former rent to calculate them against, *e.g.* where the occupier is a former service occupier or tenant, with no quantified rent element, or a trespasser. In either case, the landlord may in any event use Order 26 (or, in the High Court, Order 113): no money can be claimed in Order 26 and 113 proceedings. If a landlord uses normal proceedings and claims an amount by way of mesne profits, either the parties can agree how much ought to be paid, or the court must decide: the landlord cannot decide for himself unchallengeably. It may be worth agreeing a figure, provided this resembles a fair or reasonable rent, if an occupier is receiving Supplementary Benefit (see Chapter 7) as, if the landlord is prepared to accept the money week by week, the occupier will be able to claim a "rent element" with his benefit.

Unfortunately, many landlords will not accept such a payment, thinking that they may do their case some harm if they do. In fact, a landlord can accept a sum for use and occupation, by way of mesne profits, without inferring that a new agreement has commenced. They are more likely to do this when acting under legal advice, especially as they may be advised that they are unlikely otherwise to get any money back at all.

Some landlords try and abuse the right to accept mesne profits by serving notice and then accepting a sum which they term mesne profits, perhaps indefinitely. They might do this in order to feel completely free to start possession proceedings whenever they wish, and yet retain an income from the premises in question. This is no different from an attempt to call a tenancy a licence: the same principles apply. What was the true nature of the arrangement? Was the landlord truly accepting mesne profits while commencing or preparing for legal proceedings? Or was the landlord trying to have his cake and eat it in the way suggested?

(vi) *Costs*

At the end of a case, there may, and normally will, be an order for costs. This usually means that the winning side is entitled to reclaim his legal expenses from the loser, for example, cost of legal representation, cost of witnesses, issue of summons, etc. Sometimes, there will be a "mixed" order for costs, for example, where there are several issues, or where there has been both claim and counterclaim, in which case there may be a complex order for costs, for example that the plaintiff recovers half only of his costs and, perhaps, that the defendant can set off some of his costs against those he owes the plaintiff. When costs are finally assessed, they become a debt under a court order, just like any monetary damages that the court has ordered one side to pay to another.

Assessment of costs is by a court official, normally the registrar. The court will decide how much it is fair for one side to pay of another side's costs. This process is known as taxation. A person who has been represented by a lawyer can also query the amount of his bill by asking for taxation. Taxation is on a number of different scales. There is no comprehensive explanation for this, but the costs which one side must pay to another if the court so orders will be taxed on the "party and party" scale, which is lower than the "solicitor and client" scale appropriate to taxation of a bill from a solicitor to his own client. This means that a victorious client who recovers costs from the other side may yet have to pay his own solicitor some of the costs. The position is affected by the question of legal aid: see Appendix 2. Generally, a court will not order a legally aided client to pay more by way of costs to the other side than the client has been ordered to pay by way of contribution to his own legal aid costs. This may be different, however, if the way in which the case has been conducted suggests to the court that it ought to take a more stringent view, for example if the legally aided person's case has been constructed mainly from abuse, lies, malice, etc.

Whether or not costs are awarded is a matter of discretion for the court. It does not invariably award costs, for example, when a landlord has succeeded in claiming possession on the ground known as "greater hardship," or by the provision of suitable alternative accommodation (see Chapter 4.) It may be reluctant to add to the hardship of the soon-to-be homeless occupier, or it may, while recognising a landlord's technical entitlement to possession, for some other reason, disapprove of the landlord's conduct. This is fairly rare, however, and the loser will normally have to pay costs. If the winning party asks the court to do so, it has power to "assess" costs itself, to save the process of taxation. Costs assessed are comparatively low, *e.g.* £20/£30 plus the cost of issuing the summons.

(vii) *Warrant for possession*

If a court does order an occupier to give up possession of premises, then the landlord will normally want the court to enforce this judgement. In cases where it would be illegal to evict without due process of law (see Chapter 8) this probably means that a landlord has to use court officials to carry out the eviction. In other cases, a landlord runs the risk of committing an offence under the Criminal Law Act 1977 (see Chapter 6) if he does the evicting himself, while an occupier who is or could have been subject to Order 26/113 proceedings will commit an offence if he resists or obstructs court bailiffs. Tempers run high at evictions and there is good cause always to see that it is carried out through the officers of the court if the occupier cannot leave beforehand.

A landlord to whom a possession order has been granted can ask for it to be issued on the day that is specified in the judge's order, normally 28 days after the hearing. If no day is specified, then at least 14 days must elapse between order and issue of warrant. The landlord need only fill in an application form for the bailiff's warrant to be issued, there does not have to be a hearing before the court to decide this *unless* the court has ordered that a warrant shall not issue "without the leave of the court." This normally only happens where the court has made a suspended order, for example, on payment off the arrears, and wants to ensure that it is not enforced for trivial or even inaccurate causes. The warrant must issue within two years of judgment, or else the leave of the court will be required before it can be enforced.

Once a warrant for possession has been issued, it will remain in force until it is executed, or for one year. After one year, it automatically lapses, unless the landlord has sought an extension from the court. Execution means that a court bailiff will attend at the premises and evict the occupiers, locking up the premises and giving the key to the landlord. Although there is no requirement for bailiffs to give notice of when they propose to attend, in practice most of them do so. Once the premises have been locked up by the bailiff, possession has in law returned to the landlord and any further entry by the former occupier would be as a trespasser.

(viii) *Execution of monetary judgment*

Simply because one side has been ordered to pay money to

another does not mean that this money will be paid. There are a number of steps which may be taken in connection with enforcing the judgment. The successful party can apply for the "judgment debtor" to be examined as to his means; may ask for a charge to be put on any property of the judgment debtor, *i.e.* which means that the creditor will be able to claim the debt out of proceeds of sale; a judgment may be enforced by attachment of a person's earnings, *i.e.* stopping an amount each week out of pay at source; a person can be pushed into bankruptcy for failing to pay a judgment debt of sufficient value; it is even possible for a person refusing to pay to find himself imprisoned. All of these proceedings will only take place through further court proceedings, although these will not normally be dealt with by the judge but by a registrar or, in some cases, by another senior court official. These processes are available to either a landlord or an occupier. An occupier should always put a charge on the house property in question, to make sure that the landlord does not sell it and disappear with the proceeds before payment of the debt. On persistent failure to pay, a landlord may be forced into bankruptcy and the debt extracted from subsequent sale of the property by the trustee or official receiver.

(ix) *Committal for contempt*

If a landlord fails to obey an order of the court, for example, effectively to readmit an occupier, there may be an application to commit him for contempt of court. On an application for committal, a court can either imprison or fine the person who is in contempt, although it will usually give a recalcitrant landlord at least one further opportunity to comply. Before the court can exercise its powers, the landlord will normally need to have been given two clear days' notice of the application, although a court could dispense with this requirement and commit even without the landlord present in cases of extreme urgency. A court is highly unlikely to do this unless the matters alleged are so serious that there is a risk of injury to the occupier, in which case, in any event, a crime which the police might pay attention to may well have been committed.

Contempt of court is a fairly serious business, although it can differ in its degrees, for without obedience to court orders, the court's very purpose is under threat or even rendered valueless.

2. *The High Court*

Procedure in the High Court is not very different in outline from that in the county court, although the various stages and titles of officials may differ. The High Court has all the power and jurisdiction of the county court, and more: it can hear claims to an unlimited value, can issue declarations on any legal point to a party who can show an interest in the decision, can issue injunctions to prevent or remedy any civil breach or, indeed, any breach or likely breach of the criminal law. It can only do this last, however, with the consent of the Attorney-General. This is not as intimidating a prerequisite as it sounds as this consent can be granted by his office and, if necessary, with some speed. This might be a relevant procedure if no other cause of action can be found by an occupier to remedy some particular instance of harassment, for example, in the case of an unprotected tenant remaining in occupation after the expiry of notice to quit until such time as the court makes an order for possession, in order to preserve his position as regards rehousing. High Court proceedings are more expensive and take longer than those in the county court.

3. *The Court of Appeal*

Appeals from both county and High Court will go to the Court of Appeal (Civil Division.) There is only a limited right of appeal from the country court when the reason the appellant wishes to appeal is because he disagrees with the court's findings as to what are the true facts of the case. There is always an appeal if the argument is over whether or not the court has correctly interpreted and applied the law. Appeals are also expensive and usually take some time to be heard. Although in theory it should not be absolutely essential to have legal representation, in practice this will always be indispensible: see Appendix 2 for legal advice and assistance. An appeal from the Court of Appeal itself would lie to the House of Lords.

4. *The Divisional Court*

This is also an important court in housing law. It hears appeals on points of law only (*i.e.* not the facts) from the criminal courts. Appeals on points of fact from the magistrates courts lie to the Crown Court, and from the Crown Court to the Court of Appeal (Criminal Division.) The importance of the Divisional Court lies in its jurisdiction to supervise the work of tribunals, such as the Rent Tribunal and the Rent Assessment Committee, and public officials, such as local authorities or rent officers. An appeal from a rent officer's decision on a point of law as to whether or not he has jurisdiction over the application in question may be taken to the Divisional Court, although it could also be referred to the county court. A claim to the Divisional Court may be made in respect of, for example, a local authority, on the ground that it has acted outside its powers, or that it has refused to perform some duty, *e.g.* as regards homelessness.

The claim to the Divisional Court is not one for monetary compensation. It is for an order, by way of application for judicial review, that is in many respects like an injunction to the public body. These orders are known as the Prerogative Orders, and they are: *mandamus* (compelling the body to do something), *certiorari* (quashing an existing decision of the body) and prohibition (forbidding the body from doing something.) Sometimes more than one order will issue at the same time: *e.g.* a *certiorari* quashing a decision of the Rent Tribunal, and a *mandamus* compelling it to rehear the application. Such claims should also be undertaken, in practice, only with legal advice and assistance: see Appendix 2.

The procedure is idiosyncratic. The first stage is for an "application for leave" to be made, which states what it is that the applicant wants from the court and, by way of affidavit in support, what the facts are that give rise to his alleged entitlement. If there is on the face of it a good claim, *i.e.* without hearing the other side, then leave will be given for a full hearing, at which both sides will be represented. This full hearing may take a very long time to come up, unless there is some urgency about the matter in which case the court which grants leave will also order an "expedited hearing." It is not necessary in the course of the application to state exactly what sort of order is required. No one is ever obliged to have legal represent-ation, although this is commonly advisable. If a person is not represented by a lawyer, then he may act for himself. In some cases, in either the Court of Appeal or the Divisional Court, the court may consider the point at issue to be of such general importance that it seeks additional representation, by a govern-ment employed lawyer whose job is to represent the government on most matters, who also represents many public bodies and who intervenes as "a friend of the court" to take a particular interest whenever the court sees fit to ask for his intervention.

In the magistrates and county courts, both barristers and solicitors have a right of audience, although solicitors will normally instruct a barrister because the barrister may be more expert in the particular sort of problem, or have greater experience of advocacy, or because the solicitor does not have the time to spend the whole day at court. In the higher courts, only a barrister has right of audience from amongst the legal profession. A lay person can only instruct a barrister by first retaining a solicitor, and a barrister can normally only accept instructions to appear in a case from a solicitor.

The courts generally have discretion to allow some other person to speak for a party to an action who feels that he cannot adequately represent himself. They do not exercise this right freely or, indeed, easily at all, for fear of a body of "unqualified advocates" building up, and also because they will consider that they can assist the unrepresented client as much as is necessary. It is theoretically a part of a judge's duty to make sure that a party before the court does not suffer from lack of representation, but this it often does not discharge satisfactorily. A court may also feel easier about permitting representation if, for example, the issue is only one of terms of a suspended order, or some exercise of its discretion.

If, however, a person is not represented, then as of right he is entitled to have a friend sitting with or near to him in order to assist in the presentation of the case, *e.g.* by writing down notes or passing over questions to the unrepresented person. Such a person is known as a Mackenzie Adviser after the court decision, *Mackenzie* v. *Mackenzie*, in which this right to assistance in coping with the complexity of legal proceedings was affirmed.

In most cases, occupiers will be able to get some form of qualified advice, whether from an agency such as a Housing Aid or Action Centre, a CAB, or from a lawyer in a Law Centre, or from a lawyer in private practice. Legal assistance may constitute advice only, or it may constitute full and, if the occupier qualifies, completely free representation. This subject forms the matter of the next Appendix.

Appendix 2: Further Advice, Assistance and Information

1. *Legal Aid and Advice*

There are two forms of legal assistance which may be appropriate to any civil case. A person charged before a criminal court may be granted legal aid by the court but, because this will rarely affect an occupier as regards the law described in this book, it will not be considered further here. These forms of legal assistance entitle the occupier to approach any solicitor, not just those working through some public or quasi-public agency.

The so-called Green Form scheme permits a person to receive advice or assistance from a solicitor up to the value of £25 of that solicitor's time and work. There is a crude means test, applied by the solicitor, which determines a client's contribution. The amount of work which may be done remains the same, *i.e.* £25, whatever the contribution of the client, although a solicitor can apply to the body which administers both schemes, the Law Society, for permission to do further work than that valued at £25, up to a maximum of £200. The client's contribution is paid directly to the solicitor and forms the first part of his remuneration. For example, if a client is seen "under the Green Form" and has to pay a contribution of £15, then if that solicitor does no more than £15 worth of work, the solicitor will not claim anything from the Law Society.

The means test allows a fixed amount of capital or property ownership, and deducts from net pay fixed allowances in respect of dependents. The Green Form is appropriate for initial advice, for example, as to whether or not to defend a case, perhaps preliminary letters or some other investigations, *e.g.* a surveyor's report as to whether there is something structurally wrong with premises. The lawyer cannot take any "step in proceedings," *i.e.* either representation or the filing of one or other of the pleadings described in Appendix 1, under the Green Form. For that, he needs legal aid. However, the lawyer could advise the occupier how to take such a step on his own behalf, including telling an occupier what to say in, *e.g.* a defence. It is a very useful way of getting in to see a lawyer and find out what the position is.

Legal Aid itself is somewhat more cumbersome. It is designed to secure the representation of a solicitor and, if necessary, a barrister (or, in exceptional cases, even two barristers) in the conduct of a case, whether by a plaintiff or a defendant. Legal Aid works by the grant of a certificate, on receipt of which the solicitor works for the individual client and carries out any normal step in proceedings, but is remunerated by the Law Society. In order to get Legal Aid, there must be an application and a statement which reveals either a cause of action or a defence. There will also be a means test conducted by the Supplementary Benefits Commission on behalf of the Law Society. This will determine what, *if any*, contribution the client ought to pay towards his own expenses. These are paid, usually by instalment, to the Law Society, not to the solicitor. It is generally considered that the qualifying conditions for Legal Aid are inadequate, *i.e.* that too many people are excluded without good cause. People on Supplementary Benefit and those who are very poor do not have to pay a contribution.

Legal Aid will not normally be granted if the value in issue is not more than £200, although if, for example, the action is also for an injunction in a case of harassment or illegal eviction, this figure will not be relevant. Similarly, an application for an injunction alone, whether for harassment or eviction, or for domestic violence, will qualify for Legal Aid. It is not available in respect of certain types of action, for example, defamation, although it is in respect of all housing matters to be heard in a civil court. Legal Aid is only available normally in courts, *i.e.* not Tribunals or before the Rent Officer, nor is it available to prosecute a criminal matter.

At the end of the case, the client may be successful or otherwise. If he is successful, and there is an order for costs against the other side, the solicitor will first recover costs from the

other side. He will then be entitled to claim any balance from
the Law Society. This balance is created by the difference
allowable on taxation between party and party costs and
solicitor and own client costs: see Appendix 1. However, the
Law Society has the right to recoup any such balance out of
damages awarded to the client. It does not invariably press this
charge, *e.g.* if it would cause undue hardship. Some solicitors
do not claim from the Law Society at all in such circumstances, accepting instead only the somewhat lower figure
allowed from the other side. There is a similar charge when
Green Form work results in the recovery of money.

If the client loses the case, then costs will normally be
awarded against him. However, if he is legally aided, in
normal circumstances the court will limit the amount that the
other side can recover to the same amount as the legally aided
person's contribution. This means the client may still have to
pay his contribution twice over, *i.e.* once to the Law Society
and once to the other side. Of course, the costs of the other side
may not even amount to the full size of the contribution, which
can be extensive. If there is a nil contribution there should be
no order for costs in favour of the other side. The circumstances in which a court might abandon this presumption are
referred to in Appendix 1.

The Law Society publishes a Legal Aid Referral List of
lawyers within each district who are prepared to take work on
legal aid. They specify what sorts of work they are prepared to
do under legal aid. This specification indicates willingness to
do that type of work, not experience. Many solicitors consider
that they are prepared to, as it were, "try their hand at anything" and, consequently, check off each of the categories
listed in the Referral List. More responsible solicitors only
check off those cases they are either particularly interested or
experienced in. Most solicitors are not trained in the areas of
law known as welfare law, which includes housing from an
occupier's point of view.

2. *Advice and Aid Agencies*

There are a number of agencies which provide services free of
charge to occupiers. Of these agencies, only Law Centres

provide both full free advice and, where necessary, free representation. They all employ fully qualified lawyers. Some Law Centres do, however, use the legal aid and advice schemes and this may on occasion result in the need for a client to pay a contribution to the Law Society. Law Centres do not do all types of work, but most of them will always assist with the problems described in this book. They are generally more experienced and often better trained to do this sort of work and the quality of the advice received is usually high. They also provide a broader perspective than most solicitors will provide, e.g. by considering the matter from several angles such as the possibility of rehousing, entitlement to welfare benefits, other approaches merely than legal proceedings.

Many areas have Housing Action Centres, which are normally voluntary bodies which will advise, conduct assistance or representation in front of Tribunals or Rent Officer, but cannot conduct legal cases in the way a lawyer in private practice or a Law Centre can. There are also Housing Aid Centres which are usually funded by local authorities. The extent of their work will vary from area to area: some being no more than a "front-office" for the authority, others giving advice only, some will undertake more active work along the lines of an Action Centre.

There are Citizens Advice Bureaux in many areas, and these provide advice. Some of them will have a lawyer attached to the office who will usually provide legal backup to the lay advisers, but may see some clients himself. There are two CAB which are attached to Law Centres and which refer cases to them where necessary. Otherwise, a CAB does not normally do much more than advise the client and perhaps write a letter or two on his behalf.

Finally, there is a Surveyor's Aid Service, which operates in London only and which conducts a means test of its own. Its purpose is to assist people before Rent Tribunals, Rent Officers and Rent Assessment Committees where, as has been remarked in Chapters 4 and 5, the experience and representations of a surveyor may be of more relevance than those of a lawyer.

In addition to these aid agencies, there are lobby or pressure groups which provide a different sort of service:

Shelter, The National Campaign For The Homeless, 157 Waterloo Road, London SE1 8UU; this is a pressure group which is highly active in housing matters. Where an issue of importance is concerned, it may fund or promote a case, although its principal function is that of promoting parliamentary reform.

SHAC, The London Housing Aid Centre, 189a, Old Brompton Road, London SW5 OAN: this is Shelter's Housing Aid Centre which will provide assistance and advice within the London area as appropriate. It does not have full-time lawyers on the staff but, although called an Aid Centre, can be extremely active.

Child Poverty Action Group, 1, Macklin Street, London WC2B 5NH; this is also a pressure group, on behalf of the poor. It provides information and material about poverty, much of which is highly influential and all of which is well respected. It does not deal directly with housing, save insofar as housing-related matters can also be issues of poverty, *e.g.* heating costs, housing allowances, rent/rate rebates/ Allowances, etc.

Citizen's Rights Office, 1, Macklin Street, London WC2B 5NH: this is CPAG's advice body, which will also on occasion represent people in particular cases. It does have a full-time lawyer on the staff who is permitted to take cases in the normal way. It's principal remit is that of poverty and welfare benefits, but, again, these are issues often closely interrelated with housing.

3. *Further Reading*

(i) *Periodicals*

Legal Action Group Bulletin, published by the Legal Action Group, 28a, Highgate Road, London, NW5 1NS; this is a monthly journal of social welfare law aimed not only at lawyers but others working in the field, including, specifically, social workers and advisers. It is the only essential reading for anyone seeking to remain fully up-to-date as to housing developments from the point of view of welfare law. The Group also publishes pamphlets and other materials, including an annual list of advice and aid agencies.

Journal of Social Welfare Law, to be published in late 1978 by Sweet & Maxwell, 11 New Fetter Lane, London EC4P 4EE; this journal will also deal with social welfare law developments. It is intended to contain a great deal of useful information in the form of articles, notes of cases, notes of legislation and current practice with particular reference to the work of welfare lawyers and social workers.

Roof, published by Shelter (see above): news and views on housing, including some (but not much) housing law.

(ii) *Books*

Landlord and Tenant, Martin Partington, Weidenfeld & Nicholson; this is a general study of housing law, which sets much of it in context. It includes materials other than those drawn directly from strictly legal sources, *e.g.* statistics, debates, reports, etc. It is not a comprehensive guide to the subject, but is an excellent and valuable study which bridges housing law and housing as a sociological subject and enables the reader to see how the two interrelate.

Housing Rights Handbook, Marion Cutting, Penguin (to be published shortly): this is a lay guide to the subject of housing law. It is comprehensive and comparatively easy to read. Its purpose is simply to set out the rules, rights, duties, etc.

Index